THE GODS OF MAN

Gods of Nature - God of War

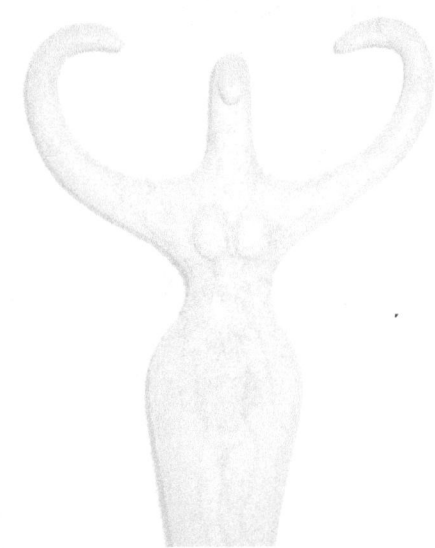

By Gary R. Varner
Member of the American Folklore Society and
the Foundation for Mythological Studies

GODS OF MAN

ISBN: 978-1-4357-0331-5

An OakChylde Book published by Lulu Press, Inc.
Visit the author's website: www.authorsden.com/garyrvarner

"Gods are rarely invented or discovered; rather they are taken over by one group from another." –Raphael Patai, *The Hebrew Goddess,* 1978

"For nearly four thousand years we have been living, intellectually at least, under the burden of an incredible deception…As soon as the cult of Yahweh triumphed, the Goddess of the Beginnings was reduced to her simplest form, and the Lilith of the rabbinical tradition, assigned to darkness." –Jean Markale, *The Great Goddess,* 1997

"…millions of people still today seem incapable of perceiving what our sacred literature really says, and how it functions to maintain the boundaries that keep us imprisoned in a dominator society." –Riane Eisler, *The Chalice & the Blade,* 1987

"But we will certainly do whatsoever thing goeth forth out of our own mouth, to burn incense unto the queen of heaven, and to pour out drink offerings unto her, as we have done, we, and our fathers, our kings, and our princes, in the cities of Judah, and in the streets of Jerusalem: for then we had plenty of victuals, and we were well, and saw no evil.

"But since we left off to burn incense to the queen of heaven, and to pour out drink offerings unto her, we have wanted all things, and have been consumed by the sword and by famine."—Jeremiah, 44: 17-18

"Orthodox Christians believe that fear is essential to sustain what they perceive to be a divinely ordained hierarchical order in which a celestial God reigns singularly at a pinnacle, far removed from earth and all humankind." –Helen Ellerbe, *The Dark Side of Christian History,* 1995

GODS OF MAN

Contents

Introduction

There probably has never been a time when thinking humans, even those that scientists do not recognize as being properly "human," have not believed in an intelligent, supernatural being or beings existing outside and independent of human culture and society.

Originally, the gods were believed to show their presence by the moving of leaves and grasses, by the sounds they made in the thunder, by the lightening, which struck the earth and caused fire. The gods were present in all things, the stones, trees, waters, mountains and clouds had spirits and rational thought and were believed to play active roles in the lives of each individual.

Trees and standing stones were said to walk at night, women were made pregnant by spirits residing in trees, stone and water. Today in some parts of the world, spirits are said to exist in bladed weapons, groves, meteors and animals. God is found in the world of nature by many and in permanent structures by many more.

Today we live in a violent world where war is constant and fought in the name of God. Peace is often invoked at the same time in the name of the same God. Tolerance is unknown by both warring factions and both believe that they will be rewarded in heaven for their acts of terror, genocide and the destruction of free will and free thought. How did humankind get to this state?

We may ask why the Judeo-Christian God that so dominates the world's religions did not exist prior to the creation of the earliest books of the Bible, around 3000 BCE? Obviously, humans had existed for hundreds of thousands, perhaps millions of years previously but this god-figure did not appear until relatively recently in the worlds history. Why? And why at that particular time in history?

This book will attempt to answer those questions by discussing the changing belief systems that humankind has had since ancient times and how the gods we worship have been altered by men through time to provide a semblance of authority for their inhumanity and domination of others.

The lotus flower pictured on the cover was chosen due to its symbolization of birth and rebirth, the origin of cosmic life and the creator gods. Attributions for the photographs in Chapter Eight and in the afterword could not be located and the author solicits information from anyone who may have information concerning their sources. Proper credit will be given in subsequent revisions.

Chapter One
Why Gods Exist

"It is the task of the Divine to condemn the errors of antiquity, and of the philologists to account for them; I will only pray you to read, with patience, and human sympathy, the thoughts of men who lived without blame in a darkness they could not dispel and to remember that, whatever charge of folly may justly attach to the saying, 'There is no God,' the folly is prouder, deeper, and less pardonable, in saying; 'There is no God but for me.'"

--John Ruskin, 1819-1900 [1]

Humankind has a need to recognize a god or gods—be they nature spirits or large and fearsome gods of terror. Early man, regardless if they were Neanderthal, Homo Erectus or Ramapithicus, experienced god as a force of nature—the rising sun, the circling moon, the continued flow of the rivers and the winds. He may have found god in one of the many fierce predators that he faced in the struggle for survival as well.

The origins of religion are perhaps tied to primal fear. "The idea," wrote Brenda Lewis, "that all misfortunes had its origin in the supernatural world—whether it was disease, drought, famine, floods, volcanic eruptions or any other calamity—was recognized wherever

---

[1] Ruskin, John. *The Queen of the Air: Being A Study of the Greek Myths of Cloud and Storm*. Chicago: Homewood Publishing Company, nd., 10

people lived close to Nature and its depredations." [2] Lewis notes, "The development of human spirituality and an understanding of violent and unpredictable Nature went hand in hand with human evolution." [3]

Fear continues to be a major factor in religion and why we embrace it. Some welcome religion as a comfort against adversity and as a protection against evil—much in the same way as our ancient ancestors did when religion was embodied in the form of an animal or nature spirit.

Lewis summed it up when she wrote, "First personalized into gods, then into more spiritual beings resembling humans, but infinitely more powerful, Nature's potential to assault and destroy has been humanity's perennial predicament." [4]

However, these early gods of nature were not only fearful but worshipped as gods of fertility, of life renewed and consistent. It is this combination, as well as a combination of the dual aspects of nature— both good and evil, that carries over into contemporary culture and how many of us view "God" today.

Because early man felt the need to credit the gods with the acts of Nature as well as his own foibles he also needed to give some responsibility to the gods for perceived evil—either the destructive

---

[2] Lewis, Brenda Ralph. *Ritual Sacrifice: Blood and Redemption*. Phoenix Mill: Sutton Publishing Limited 2006, 1.

[3] Ibid., vii.

[4] Ibid., 1.

actions of Nature or the anti-social and violent acts of fellow men. In Christianity this was the doing of Satan, a god of evil—the fallen angel who wished to usurp the kingdom of God.

However, "evil" at one time was regarded as part of the dual aspect of the universe and was a creation of God. Evil in the Old Testament was not assigned to demons but as a logical conclusion that if God created all then he also created evil along with good. "…for if we credit God with all Good things, we must also credit him with Evil ones". [5] As Anthony Mercatante noted, "…in the Old Testament there is no concept of demons in the sense of preternatural powers that can intervene in man's life; the Old Testament attributes all man's misfortunes to God, not to demons." [6]

One specific passage in the Old Testament makes it quite clear that evil arises not from Satan but from God:

"I form the light, and create darkness: I make peace, and create evil: I the Lord do all these things." [7]

This was a common belief of most early religions and one that caused the need for regular propitiations and sacrifice to pacify the gods. It was also this belief that contributed to the belief that the gods took sides and could be persuaded to align themselves with nations and to annihilate their enemy, i.e., "God is on our side." This belief continues to this day and is used often by political leaders and in

---

[5] Mercantante, Anthony S. *Good and Evil in Myth & Legend.* New York: Barnes & Noble Books 1996, 4.
[6] Ibid.
[7] Isaiah 45: 7

churches when priests and ministers request God to fight against "terrorists" and other perceived enemies as well as against gays, Wiccans and others not in the mainstream of society.

We may wonder how the pantheons of gods, goddesses and demigods originated in ancient times. Until recent years, the comfortable theory of human evolution has said that sedentary villages with their associated burials, temples, agriculture and hearths began around 8500 BCE during the Neolithic period. Gradually this scenario has changed in the face of archaeological anomalies, which occurred more and more frequently that indicates human evolution began much earlier with technological and social advancements. A recent article in Minerva Magazine [8] by professor Helmut Ziegert of Hamburg University illustrates the changing mind set of archaeologist today. According to Ziegert, Homo Erectus as long ago as 900,000 years BCE had mastered trans-oceanic travel and had sedentary villages dating back to 400,000 years. Such villages included cemeteries. Homo Erectus, says Dr. Ziegert, "was socially more akin to modern humans than to his primitive predecessors."

The very existence of cemeteries 900,000 years in age indicates that humankind has believed in a need to care for the deceased. Such care may indicate that a belief in the continuation of the spirit after death, i.e. "life after death," existed. In addition, such evidence may exist that

---

[8] Ziegert, Helmut. "A New Dawn for Humanity: Lower Palaeolithic Village Life in Libya and Ethiopia", in Minerva –The International Review of Ancient Art & Archaeology, July/August 2007 (Vol 18.4)

these very early humans practiced "ancestor worship" as a precursor of worshipping a deity or deities. Ancestor worship has been overused as a term of explanation for early religious practice, however. John S. Mbiti, Professor of Religious Studies at Makerere University, wrote the following concerning ancestor worship:

"...the departed, whether parents, brothers, sisters, or children, form part of the family, and must therefore be kept in touch with their surviving relatives. Libation and the giving of food to the departed are tokens of fellowship, hospitality and respect; the drink and food so given are symbols of family continuity and contact." [9]

Ancestor worship, according to Mbiti, is only one small segment of any "primitive" religion. If we agree that Homo Erectus established cemeteries, worshipped his ancestors or at least was concerned with their well-being after death, we must also agree that he had a concept of a deity that was tied directly to nature, the acts of nature, and the continuation of existence.

To early man the most fearsome threat to his existence was the predatory animals that lived alongside of him. These animals played an important part in Paleolithic ritual and religion. It is this which is the earliest evidence of religion.

One of the earliest and finest examples of prehistoric art depicting an animal in a god-like image was created approximately 32,000 years

---

[9] Mbiti, John S. *African Religions and Philosophy*. New York: Anchor Books 1969, 11.

ago and placed in the Hohlenstein Stadel Cave in southern Germany. Carved from a mammoths tusk, this statue, almost 30 cm in height, portrays a being with a man's body and a lions head. Other animal-headed figures have been found at Chauvet Cave in France. This statue was a hybrid figure with a man's body and a bison's head. It is interesting during this time that images of the male always included these man-animal figures but women were always portrayed realistically.

The famous drawings of "sorcerers" obviously reflect a supernatural image. One of these, known as the "Horned God" found at Trois Frères, France "combines the beard, legs and feet of a human being, the antlers and ears of a deer, the face of an owl, the tail of a horse and the sexual organs of a lion."[10]

Current archaeological theory is that these ancient images were used to convey religious "signs" to initiates. These images conveyed the fear and awe felt by early man as well as the power that was inherent in these animals. Animal-men that were worshipped as the dual aspect of nature. By "becoming" part of these powerful beings men were able to feel that they had some control over nature, that they shared in the spiritual being of the gods. They also were able to feel that they had some interactive influence with the supernatural and could call upon it in need.

---

[10] Mohen, Jean-Pierre. *Prehistoric Art: The Mythical Birth of Humanity*. Paris: Telleri 2002, 139.

Nowhere else was the development of hybrid gods more eloquent than in ancient Egypt. However, these gods appear to have been universally regarded throughout the world and throughout various times. They are found in Native American rock art and mythology, Australia, throughout Asia, Africa and Europe. Are these, perhaps, the remnants of an ancient and primordial religion that at one time united humankind?

Many of the hybrid Egyptian gods and goddesses, such as Anubis shown below, are known to have originated before the beginning of recorded time and may date back to the time when hybrid gods took shape in the Paleolithic. The lion-headed god which was beautifully represented in the 32,000 year old statue discussed above from Germany is mimicked in Egyptian art from the Greco-Roman period.

The hybrid god has existed in human culture for at least 32,000 years and possibly for another 900,000 years. Hybrid gods most likely were chosen because the actual animal they represent is a dangerous one or one that could offer protection.

Another Egyptian hybrid god, Bastet, the cat. Originally a lioness deity, she is also linked to the underworld as the protector of the dead.

In regards to Egyptian gods, according to Egyptologists Lorna Oakes and Lucia Gahlin, "another consideration appears to have been that, by depicting a deity in the form of a dangerous animal such as the snake (for example, the fertility goddess Renenutet or Mertseger, the patron deity of the west Theban peak), and then by worshipping that deity, the animal in question might in turn be placated and the hazard allayed." [11]

In addition, many of the animals were believed to have protective powers and their images were used to ward off harm and evil.

---

[11] Oakes, Lorna and Lucia Gahlin. *Ancient Egypt*. New York: Barnes & Noble Books 2006, 269.

Undoubtedly, these same considerations played into the early forms of Paleolithic religion as well.

The gradual transition of animal gods to anthropomorphic (human-like) gods is explained by Sir James Frazer. According to Frazer, many of the ancient animal gods that humans worshipped became figures of sacrifice in later times. For example, followers of Mithras were baptized in bull's blood. Scenes of bull-slayings, according to D. Jason Cooper, were "meant to encompass the whole of the religion's teachings." [12] Such images, according to Cooper, "defines the religion more closely than the crucifix, the Star of David, and the crescent define Christianity, Judaism, and Islam respectively." [13]

And who slays the bull? Mithras, of course. Similar religious symbols exist in other ancient religions as well. Dionysus, god of wine and vegetation was also known as "eater of bulls" and he is often represented eating raw goat's blood. Dionysus is himself the slayer. In ancient Egypt Apis, [14] the bull, was slain annually. Perhaps regarded as the most sacred of all animals, the slain bull was mummified and buried with the same ceremony, as a pharaoh would receive.

In all of these examples the sacrificed animal was, at an earlier time, the god. In the case of Dionysus and Mithras the symbolism is

---

[12] Cooper, D. Jason. *Mithras: Mysteries and Initiation Rediscovered.* York Beach: Samuel Weiser, Inc. 1996, 59.
[13] Ibid.
[14] Apis was the manifestation of the Creator God of Memphis, Ptah.

that the god sacrifices himself. Apis, being the earthly representation of Ptah, the Creator, is also sacrificed so that creation can be renewed.

Mithras slaying the bull.

Similar sacrifices were common among the Jews as well. According to scholar E.O. James, "The priest was to sacrifice a bullock for a sin-offering for himself and the rest of the priesthood and a ram for a burnt-offering. Then he was to 'set before Yahweh' two he-goats. Lots were cast upon them to determine which was to be assigned to Yahweh as a sin-offering, and which was to be presented to a goat demon, Azazel, as the sin-receiver." [15] By conducting such a sacrifice, life would continue for the Jews with their sins washed away by the goat's blood.

---

[15] James, E.O. *The Ancient Gods*. Edison: Castle Books 2004, 155.

Bulls were sacrificed annually in Iceland at the assembly of the Icelandic Parliament, known as the Althing, until 1000 CE when Christianity took hold but continued in secrecy by decree of the Althing.

Evidence of ancient animal sacrifices have been found in several caves in Europe, most notably at Drachenlock in Switzerland where bear skulls had been arranged by Neanderthals in such as way that magic and ritual are indicated. In southern France, the skulls and bones of as many as twenty bears were arranged in a rectangular pit, which had been sealed with a stone slab weighing one ton. Bear sacrifice continues into the 21st century among the Ainu of Japan—the indigenous people of that country. Many archaeologists believe that bear worship was practiced among the Neanderthal and that the bear's sacrifice was an extension of that worship.

In many ways, these ancient expressions of sacrifice have continued into contemporary society and religious practice. While these early sacrifices reflected the belief in sacrificing the god, so that life is renewed, contemporary Christian practice incorporate similar ritual in the communion. The ritual drinking of the "blood of Christ" as represented by the communal wine and the eating of the flesh of Christ by consuming the bread or cracker are symbolic of this ritual cannibalization of the god. The crucifixion itself is comparable with this ritual killing of the god. Carl Jung, in comparing the mysteries of Mithras with the Christian mysteries wrote "The representations of the sacrificial act, the tauroctony (bull slaying), recall the crucifixion between two thieves, one whom is raised up to paradise while the other goes down to hell."

It should be noted that these ritual sacrifices only result in the temporary death of the god's body but not of the god itself and, in fact, the god is usually instrumental in his own sacrifice as evidenced by the death of Odin, Mithras, Dionysus and Jesus and other savior gods. The Christian sacrament is, according to 19th century scholar Kersey Graves, "copied, or reproduced (from) an old pagan rite as part of his (Jesus') professedly new and spiritual system, one of the most ancient and widely-extended formulas of pagandom." [16]

Gods exist for the comfort of their creators. This is not to say that a supreme force, an intelligence, a creative-destructive being does not exist but the gods that have been fashioned since Paleolithic days are created in a way that comforts the mind, that allows humans to explain events, to seek revenge, to pass on the faults of ones own to another supernatural being that has control over ones life and destiny. That these gods originated as animal-human hybrids is indicative of the time when humans or human-like creatures first obtained a glimpse of the unknown and the powers that existed outside of man's control.

---

[16] Graves, Kersey. *The World's Sixteen Crucified Saviors.* Kempton: Adventures Unlimited Press 2001, 200. A reprint of the 1875 publication.

Chapter Two
The Creation of Supernatural Beings

How did god, the angels and demons originate anyway? In ancient history, these supernatural creatures began as animal deities. Eventually they evolved into the Earth Mother Goddess and Father God, Satan and his demons and eventually as the dominating and all-powerful Father figure, we all know today.

Animals were both food and mystery to early humans. Feared, hunted and worshipped, they were, according to Mohen, "inarticulate beings who are nonetheless the possessors of magical powers, keepers of the secrets of the forest and the personification of the invisible forces of nature." [17]

Let us review some of these animal-gods and determine how such a metamorphosis occurred.

The Bird Gods

The bird, at once powerful and majestic in flight and fragile on land has been worshipped as a god from Egypt to North America to Easter Island. "Coming from the sky", writes Buffie Johnson, "the bird portrays not only the spirit of life but also the human soul." [18]

---

[17] Mohen, Jean-Pierre. *Prehistoric Art: The Mythical Birth of Humanity*. Paris: Telleri 2002, 175.
[18] Johnson, Buffie. *Lady of the Beasts*. Rochester: Inner Traditions International 1994, 8.

Hybrid-bird-human paintings from prehistory, according to Jack Tresidder, "symbolize the spiritual side of human nature and, by implication, the promise of immortality." [19] Because of the bird's beauty, lightness and ability to fly from the earth to the heavens, gradually people began to think that the bird also represented the human soul.

Some of the birds held sacred include the Lammergeier, or sheep vulture, the falcon, the owl, the swallow, the raven, the dove, swan and the ibis.

The bird has often been associated with the soul, the spirit, and the ability to communicate with the divine. In Native American culture the Thunderbird is the Creator , the Great Universal Spirit. The Harpie, that strange Human-Bird hybrid being, is associated with the Dark, Destructive powers of nature.

The ancient Greeks personified the savage winds and storms as Harpies, creatures with the faces of women and the bodies of vultures who could create whirlpools at sea and fierce windstorms on land. They were known to swoop down from the skies, taking away anything in their paths, including buildings, trees, animals and even people.

The Harpies sole purpose was to inflict punishment upon humans, sent by the gods to cause sudden and early death. Because of their role in death, they were also known as messengers to the underworld, and

---

[19] Tresidder, Jack. *Symbols and their Meanings*. New York: Barnes & Noble 2006, 68.

as the transporters of the souls of the dead. Biedermann wrote that another duty of the Harpy was to "catch criminals and turn them over to the Fates for punishment." He further notes, "although the Harpies serve the greater moral order, they are figures of dread." [20]

Are the Harpies purely a Greek creation? No, Harpies, or Harpy-like creatures were known in ancient Mesopotamia as well. "Some Babylonian poems" note Jeremy Black and Anthony Green, "describe the dead as clothed with bird-like plumage. {The underworld} is peopled by a horde of unpleasant demons, described in graphic detail. In almost all cases, these hellish demons are said to have been winged and to have had talons of birds..." [21]

The original account of the Harpies says that they were orphan children of Poseidon (or Neptune) and Gaia, or Thaumas and Electra but they were raised by Aphrodite. When they matured, Aphrodite left them to find husbands for them but the Storm Winds, the Harpyiai, swept them from the earth and they themselves came to be Storm Winds. The Harpies had individual names meaning "squall", "fast flier", and "obscure". The name, "Harpies", is derived from the Greek "harpazein", meaning, "to snatch or carry away." [22] Other scholars say that the Harpies "delight in drinking the blood of men slain in battle",

---

[20] Biedermann, Hans. *Dictionary of Symbolism: Cultural Icons & The Meanings Behind Them*. New York: Meridian Books 1994, 39.

[21] Black, Jeremy and Anthony Green. *Gods, Demons and Symbols of Ancient Mesopotamia*. Austin: University of Texas Press 1992, 43.

[22] Andrews, Tamra. *A Dictionary of Nature Myths*. Oxford: Oxford University Press 1998, 89.

[23] much like the Celtic warrior-goddess, the Morrigin—who also appeared in the guise of a raven.

Ancient Greek carving of a Harpy, carrying away an infant.
(British Museum)

J.E. Cirlot wrote, "At a deeper level, they have been defined as a representation of the 'evil harmonies of cosmic energies'." [24] Other bird-like creatures that various cultures have attributed the creation of winds include the Garuda bird of India, the Native American

[23] Fiske, John. *Myths and Myth-Makers: Old Tales and Superstitions Interpreted by Comparative Mythology*. Boston: Houghton, Mifflin and Company 1881, 164.
[24] Cirlot, J.E.*A Dictionary of Symbols*. 2nd ed., New York: Barnes & Noble Books 1995, 139.

Thunderbird, and the Hraesvelgre of Scandinavia. The wind deities that are responsible for destruction by tornadoes, volcanoes and other violent tempests are, according to Andrews, "predominantly male, robust and fearsome and full of raw energy." [25] Like most all aspects of nature and nature deities, the winds could be either good or evil—thus displaying the dual quality of life and nature's experience. Large birds, like the Thunderbird, are often representations of thunder and wind gods.

To most indigenous people the eagle and the raven are two of the most important creatures in existence. In the Welsh triads, the "Trioedd Ynys Prydein", the eagle and the raven are two of the three oldest animals in the world. The third is the owl. The eagle is representative of divine beings, theological concepts, spirit guardians, and lofty ideals. The raven, because it is a "talking" bird, is closely linked to prophecy and wisdom. It is also, on the other hand, associated with war, destruction and death. Sailors especially saw evil in the raven. According to Anne Ross, "…a raven landing on the mast was a sure indication of witchcraft". Horseshoes were nailed to the mast to ward off the potential threat from witches, fairies and the Evil Eye. [26]

The eagle is symbolic of strength, freedom, release, royalty, authority, inspiration and spiritual principle. It is also symbolic of all of

---

[25] Andrews, op cit., 226.
[26] Ross, Anne. *Folklore of the Scottish Highlands.* Gloucestershire: Tempus Publishing LTD. 2000, 101.

the sky gods of humankind as well as the solar disc. It is, according to Walker, the "classic soul-bird…associated with the sun god, fire, and lightning." [27] The eagle appears on the Mexican flag with a snake in its talons depicting spiritual victory over evil. The eagle represents all that is good while the serpent represents all that is evil—thusly the two are symbolic of the sum total of all that is. The image of the eagle victorious over the serpent was also present in Greek symbolism. In Homer's *Illiad,* the Greek priest Kalchas observed an eagle slowly flying in the sky with a bleeding snake in its talons.

"The heavenly bird ravaging the serpent," wrote Heinrich Zimmer, "symbolized to him the victory of the patriarchal, masculine, heavenly order of the Greeks over the female principle of Asia and Troy."[28] The various mythic tales of the eagle and the serpent reflect the change in religious power from the conversion of the ancient goddess religion to the, possibly violent, usurpation of the patriarchal Sky God. Zimmer sums up the two in his book *Myths and Symbols in Indian Art*: "The eagle represents this higher, spiritual principle, released from the bondage of matter and soaring into the supreme divine being above them. On the other hand, the serpent is life-force in the sphere of life-matter. The snake is supposed to be of tenacious vitality; it rejuvenates itself by sloughing off its skin."[29]   In Native American symbolism, the eagle

---

[27] Walker, Barbara. *The Women's Encyclopedia of Myths and Secrets*. Edison: Castle Books 1996, 262.

[28] Zimmer, Heinrich. *Myths and Symbols in Indian Art and Civilization*. Princeton: Princeton University Press-Bollinger Series VI, 1946, 74.

[29] Zimmer, op cit 75.

represents the Thunder Bird, the "Universal Spirit"—the "mediator between sky and earth." [30]

Thunder Birds were gigantic creatures that created storms, sometimes violent storms, by the beating of their wings and by the shooting of lightning from their eyes and wings. Thunder Birds were, at times, beneficial to man as they brought the rain. However, they were more often than not viewed as responsible for the destruction created by these storms.

According to D'Alviella, "The Greeks, like all the Indo-European nations, seem to have figured to themselves the light of the storm under the form of a bird of prey. When they had received the image of the Thunderbolt from Asia Minor, they placed it in the talons of the eagle, and made it the scepter, and even the symbol, of Zeus...it was, said they, the eagle that brought the Thunderbolt to Zeus, when the latter was preparing to fight the Titans." [31]

The eagle has been a symbol of Pan, who gave it up to Zeus; it was a symbol to Odin and Mithras, and to St. John and to the sons of Horus. The eagle is a vehicle for the Indian god Vishnu and is the lightning bearer for Jupiter. It is also one of the four beasts of the Apocalypse and is one of the aspects of the Babylonian god Marduk and the Celtic god Lug. Zeus and Odin took the form of an eagle in their mythic pursuits but so did Jesus, at least in some Gnostic

---

[30] Cooper, J.C. *An Illustrated Encyclopaedia of Traditional Symbols.* London: Thames and Hudson 1978, 58.
[31] D'Alviella, Count Goblet. *The Migration of Symbols.* New York: University Books 1956, 98.

writings. "I manifest myself in the form of an eagle," Jesus says in the Secret Book of John, "upon the Tree of Knowledge...". [32]

In Late Post Classic Central Mexico, the fierce harpy eagle symbolized the sun as well as human sacrifice. It was an important figure to the Olmecs, Aztecs and Mayan cultures.

Large birds, in particularly eagles and vultures, were used as religious ritual objects and as offerings. Gimbutas noted that 88% of bird bones discovered in megalithic tombs in Orkney, Scotland were from white-tailed eagle. She believed that the bones "must have been an offering to the Goddess of Death, who in the Scottish islands manifested herself not as a vulture...but as other large birds with awe-inspiring wingspreads..."[33]

Among the Siberian Yakut the eagle is considered to be the creator of the "first shaman" and is also known as the Supreme Being. The Supreme Being is normally depicted as a two-headed eagle. An important relationship between the eagle and the sacred tree, usually a birch, also exists. It is this sacred tree which houses the souls of future shamans. [34] Among the Yakut people the eagle is itself a symbol of the vocation of shamanism.

---

[32] Doresse, Jean. *The Secret Books of the Egyptian Gnostics*. New York: MJF Books 1986, 207.
[33] Gimbutas, Marija. *The Language of the Goddess*. San Francisco: HarperSanFrancisco 1991, 189.
[34] Eliade, Mircea. *Shamanism: Archaic Techniques of Ecstasy*. Princeton University Press 1964, 70.

Double-headed eagle images were important in other areas of the world as well. The Hapsburg German Empire's emblem was that of the double-headed eagle as was that of the ancient Hittite empire.

Eagles were also companions and assistants to gods. Hino, the thunder god of the Iroquois, had two eagle helpers. One of the eagles, called Oshadagea, carried a lake of dew on its back so that it could sprinkle the world and save it from the attacks of Fire Spirits. [35]

While most cultures view the eagle as noble and sacred, if not outright divine, a few do look upon this bird of prey with disdain. Welsh folklore says, "if eagles of Snowden hovered over the plains their visit would be followed by disease and death." [36]

To the Plains Indians eagles "are seen as important messengers between man and the Sacred Mystery, partly because they can fly into the pure, rarefied air where the sacred can communicate with them away from the contaminating influences of earth." [37]

The raven has a long tradition in religious lore as well. Because the raven is regarded more as a carrion bird than a bird of prey, it is viewed as a deity of war and death rather than of life and lofty spiritual ideals. "There is also," writes Davidson, "the image of birds receiving and rejoicing over sacrificial victims, particularly the raven." [38] The raven is

---

[35] Andrews, Tamra. *A Dictionary of Nature Myths.* Oxford: Oxford University Press 1998, 92.

[36] Radford, Edwin and Mona A. *Encyclopaedia of Superstitions.* New York: Philosophical Library 1949, 108.

[37] St. Pierre, Mark and Tilda Long Soldier. *Walking in the Sacred Manner.* New York: Touchstone Books 1995, 111.

[38] Davidson, H.R. Ellis. *Myths and Symbols in Pagan Europe: Early Scandinavian and Celtic Religions.* Syracuse: Syracuse University Press 1988, 98.

closely associated with Irish battle-goddesses and the Norse valkyries. However, as noted, because it is a "talking bird" it has vast powers of prophecy and wisdom.

"Both Lug and Odin," wrote Davidson "were associated with the crow and the raven, the birds of the battlefield. Odin's two ravens brought him tidings every day, presumably from the battles of the world…" [39] The raven is also closely associated with the Celtic deities Macha (which means "Raven"), Morrigan and Babd—all which take the raven form. Green notes that "In the Mabinogion, ravens are beneficient otherworld creatures…but their magico-divine function is Irish legend is usually concerned with war and destruction." [40] Caches of raven figures have been found throughout Britain and they may represent an underworld aspect of the Celtic sky-god (Jupiter).

Over time, the raven had become almost synonymous with death and various superstitious beliefs became associated with it. "The raven, for instance" wrote Lady Wilde, "has a world-wide reputation as the harbinger of evil and ill-luck."[41] In some cultures, the raven was not necessarily the symbol of death but it was the symbol of the human soul. According to the Radford's "the Bororos of Brazil believe that the human soul has the shape of a bird, and passes out of the body in that form—and they favour ravens." [42] To the ancient Egyptians every

---

[39] Ibid, 90-91.
[40] Green, Miranda. *The Gods of the Celts*. Gloucester: Alan Sutton 1986, 187-188.
[41] Wilde, Lady. *Irish Cures, Mystic Charms & Superstitions*. New York: Sterling Publishing Co., Inc 1991, 92.
[42] Radford, op cit. 199.

human soul, called the *ba*, was in the form of a human-headed bird, which would fly from the body after death and travel to the after life. In Indian religion the raven was also the form that fleeing souls would take after the body had died. Even King Arthur was believed to have transformed into a raven after his death and it was common practice to tip ones hat to a raven out of respect to the great king. In Cornwall, it was a prohibition to kill any raven because, according to the superstition, "to shoot a raven is to shoot King Arthur."

In Siberian culture the raven guides the souls of the dead to the underworld.

Even though the raven is closely linked to death and war, and thusly was incorporated in battle ritual, it was also part of fertility rites and thereby with life.

Many of the goddesses that shape-shifted to the form of a raven show their dual natures through the other animal forms that they take as well. The Morrigan, the goddess of war and death, commonly changed from her raven aspect to that of a water serpent. The Celtic Raven-Goddess was also seen as a maternal figure, with nurture of both humans and the animal kingdom being her purpose.

The raven, however, has more to offer. In the Pacific Northwest Native Americans regarded the raven as a trickster and as the bringer of light and fire. To the Inuit the raven was said to have originated in the primeval darkness of creation but stayed to teach humans the knowledge they would need to succeed in the world. Ravens are also associated with fairies .and are believed to act as guardians of the Fairy treasures housed in the underworld.

. It is odd to think that such a creature became the symbol of the Christian church for those who refused a Christian burial and as "a feeder on corruption." [43]

One of humankind's oldest goddess figures is that of the bird. "In many Bronze Age myths," wrote Anne Baring and Jules Cashford, "the cosmic egg of the universe was laid by the Cosmic Mother Bird, and its cracking open was the beginning of time and space." [44]

Images of the bird goddess were common during the Neolithic as well. The dove has been associated with Inanna, goddess of Sumer, Egypt's Isis, Aphrodite of ancient Greece, and into Christianity as a symbol of the Holy Spirit.

During the Neolithic, the bird goddess was believed to be responsible for rain and the continued fertility that it brought. "The bird was the life of the waters, the epiphany of the goddess as the deep watery abyss of cosmic space as the seas and rivers, the underground wells and streams." [45] Because the bird both swam on the water and flew into space, it was a link between the earth and the heavens.

Images of the bird goddess were created for more than 25,000 years, from the 13th to the 5th millennium BCE. In Egypt's early pre-

[43] Saunders, Nicholas J. *Animal Spirits*. London: Duncan Baird Publishers 1997,117.
[44] Baring, Anne and Jules Cashford. *The Myth of the Goddess: Evolution of An Image*. London: Arkana/Penguin Books 1993, 13.
[45] Ibid., 58.

dynastic period of 4000 BCE, called the Naquada period, statues, carvings and petroglyph images of the "dancing goddess" were created. The "dancing goddess" is a hybrid image of a bird-female form with the hands over the head in a dancing or flying motion. Similar images during the same time period were made in the Minoan and Malta cultures indicating a cultural exchange between Egypt and the Mediterranean societies.

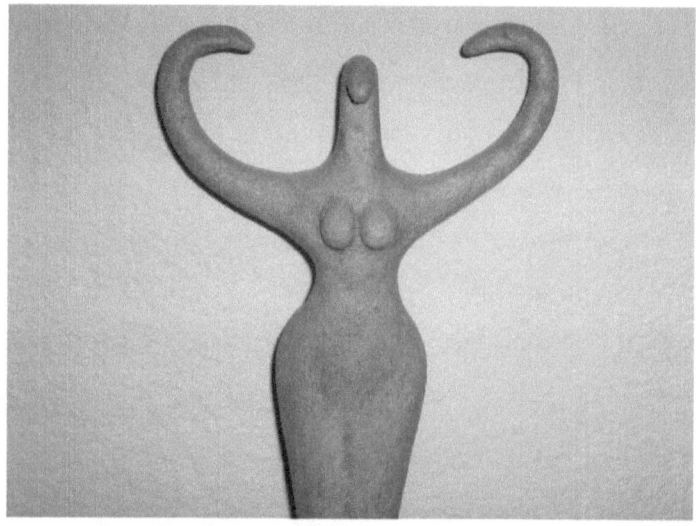

Statuette of the "dancing" Bird Goddess—goddess of fertility and rebirth.

During this period, the manifestation of divinity in animal form began its rapid evolution in Egyptian culture. Bird divinities appeared throughout history, exhibiting them around the world and culminating in the Easter Islands with the Bird Cult, which was practiced until the 1860's. The most important ritual on Easter Island was conducted to honor Makemake, the creator god who appeared as a bird-man.

The Church still recognizes these ancient goddesses to a certain degree. Philippe Walter notes, "All that the Middle Ages preserved of these bird-goddesses were saints with one goose foot. The Church either has minimized the importance of these odd female figures or has simply relegated them to anonymity." [46]

The importance of animals as representing the gods and goddesses is indicated at the beginning of Egypt's historic period when the earliest known kings of Egypt took on such names as "Kite," "Cobra," "Catfish," "Scorpion" and "Wing-spreader."

Other animals assumed the position of god as well—especially the serpent.

"The snake is a main image of the vitality and continuity of life," wrote anthropologist Marija Gimbutas, "the guarantor of life energy in the home, and the symbol of family and animal life." [47] The snake means something different and yet the same in many cultures and locations. The serpent is a feared goddess of the river, a messenger and spirit being of Native America, a water spirit and god of Africa. These are similar characteristics for a universally important symbol. There is an opposite view, however. The snake is also portrayed as Satan himself in Biblical lore. As historian Jean Markale wrote, "Western religious thought has been almost unanimous in making the serpent of Genesis into a concrete representation of the tempter, that is to say, of

[46] Walter, Philippe. *Christianity: The origins of a Pagan Religion*. Rochester: Inner Traditions 2006, 82.
[47] Gimbutas, Marija. *The Civilization of the Goddess: The World of Old Europe*. San Francisco: HarperSanFrancisco 1991, 236.

Satan himself, relying for support upon the Apocalypse where this 'great serpent'…is the image of absolute evil." [48] The serpent had been respected as a symbol of wisdom and life renewed for thousands of years—until the Hebrews and then the Christians waged successful campaigns to destroy it. "When the Hebrews introduced a male god into Canaan," says Mark O'Connell and Raje Airey, "the female deity and the snake were relegated and associated with evil." [49] Later, the Christian campaign was able to, as Page Bryant wrote, "distort a positive and ancient pagan symbol to suit the purposes of Christianity." [50]

Even before Christianity established a toehold, however, the serpent was viewed by the Hebrews as either possessed by Satan or was Satan himself. In Jewish folklore, the original serpent walked on two legs, talked and ate the same food that Adam and Eve did. One day the serpent witnessed Adam and Eve engaged in sexual relations, and he became jealous—persuading Eve to eat the forbidden fruit. In punishment, according to Hebrew legend, "its hands and legs were cut off, so it had to crawl on its belly, all food it ate tasted of dust, and it became the eternal enemy of man." [51] However, the serpent also was able to have sexual relations with Eve before he was punished by God.

---

[48] Markale, Jean. *The Great Goddess: Reverence of the Devine Feminine From the Paleolithic to the Present.* Rochester: Inner Traditions 1999, 6.

[49] O'Connell, Mark and Raje Airey. *The Complete Encyclopedia of Signs & Symbols.* London: Hermes House 2005, 186.

[50] Bryant, Page. *Awakening Arthur!* London: The Aquarian Press 1991, 64

[51] Unterman, Alan. *Dictionary of Jewish Lore & Legend.* New York: Thames and Hudson 1991, 176.

Because of this, the Israelites only became purified when they stood at Mt. Sinai and received the torah. "Gentiles, however," according to Alan Untermann, "have never been cleansed of this serpentine impurity." [52]

Christian hatred of the serpent was not universal however. In Armenian folklore, according to Anthony S. Mercatante, "Christ himself is identified with Shahapet, a beneficient serpent spirit who inhabited olive trees and vinestocks in the ancient mythology." [53]

A graven image of a serpent suspended from a cross-like beam was erected by Moses to protect the Hebrews from the poisonous bite of serpents. Acting on God's instructions, "...Moses made a serpent of brass, and put it upon a pole, and it came to pass, that if a serpent had bitten any man, when he beheld the serpent of brass, he lived." [54]

On the base of one of the ancient menhirs in Carnac is an image of five snakes standing on their tails. "When the site was excavated," writes archaeologist Johannes Maringer, "in 1922, five axes were found under the engravings. The blades faced upward; obviously the axes had been deliberately placed in that position. It is most likely that even in Neolithic times the serpent was a symbol of life." [55] Maringer believes that the serpent was closely associated with deceased ancestors and the

---

[52] Ibid.

[53] Mercatante, Anthony S. *Good and Evil in Myth & Legend.* New York: Barnes & Noble 1978, 65.

[54] Numbers 21:9, KJV

[55] Maringer, Johannes. *The Gods of Prehistoric Man: History of Religion.* London: Phoenix Press 2002, 170-171.

five serpents engraved on the menhir probably indicated that five people were buried there along with the axes.

The duality of meanings most likely originated in the contrasting views of the serpent in Old European and Indo-European mythology. In Old European lore (prior to 4500 BCE) the serpent was benevolent, a symbol of life and fertility in both plants and animals (including humans), protective of the family and of domestic livestock. "Snakes are guardians of the springs of life and immortality," wrote Spanish scholar J.E. Cirlot, "and also of those superior riches of the spirit that are symbolized by hidden treasure." [56] The poisonous snake in Old European lore was, according to Gimbutas, "an epiphany of the Goddess of Death". [57] Indo-European mythology (evolving between 4000 and 2500 BCE) contrasted this view, regarding the snake as a symbol of evil, an epiphany of the God of Death, and an adversary of the Thunder God. This was the point in time that the Goddess religion began to give way to that of the male dominated religion of the Sky God.

Gimbutas goes on to say, "it is not the body of the snake that was sacred, but the energy exuded by this spiraling or coiling creature which transcends its boundaries and influences the surrounding world." [58]

---

[56] Cirlot. J. E. *A Dictionary of Symbols, 2nd Edition*. New York: Barnes & Noble Books 1995, 286.
[57] Gimbutas, op cit, 400.
[58] Gimbutas, Marija. *The Language of the Goddess*. San Francisco: HarperSanFrancisco 1991, 121.

In the Classic world the serpent was the creator of the universe, it laid the Cosmic Egg and split it asunder to form the heavens and the earth. As Hans Leisgang wrote, "This serpent, which coiled round the heavens, biting its tail, was the cause of solar and lunar eclipses. In the Hellenistic cosmology, this serpent is assigned to the ninth, starless spheres of the planets and the zodiac. This sphere goes round the heavens and the earth and also under the earth, and governs the winds." [59] "In Christian theology," Leisegang continues, "this serpent became the prince of the world, the adversary of the transcendental God, the dragon of the outer darkness, who has barred off this world from above, so that it can be redeemed only by being annihilated." [60]

This creator-serpent, the Great Serpent, was symbolic of the sun, not evil but "the good spirit of light" as Leisegang so aptly describes it. It is this Great Serpent that is cause and ruler of the four seasons, the four winds and the four quarters of the cosmos.

A white snake, like the salmon, was a source for wisdom and magical power and was associated with the goddess/Saint Brigit, also known in England and Scotland as Bride. On February 1st, Bride's Day the serpent woke for its winter hibernation to bring in the change in seasons from winter to spring. Mackinzie relates an old Gaelic charm:

"To-day is the day of Bride,

The serpent shall come from his hole;

---

[59] Leisegang, Hans. "The Mystery of the Serpent" in *Pagan and Christian Mysteries: Papers from the Eranos Yearbook*, edited by Joseph Campbell. New York: The Bollingen Foundation/Harper & Row Publishers 1955, 26-27.
[60] Ibid, 27.

I will not molest the serpent

And the serpent will not molest me."[61]

The many serpent-like symbols found in ancient rock art the world over testify to the importance of this animal in the human mind. The zigzag and meandering lines symbolic of water, the mysterious spirals found the world over which mimic the coiled serpent all speak of the underlying mystery that humans have felt towards the snake and the snakes place in the mythos of the Otherworld and death. However, not only death, for many the snake represented life and the renewal of life. The snake was the feared guardian of life and the forces of life as well as the messenger to and from the world of the dead. Snakes were believed to be symbolic of the departed soul to the ancient Greeks. It was also valued as a guardian of temples, treasuries and oracles, its eyesight believed to be especially keen to allow it to effectively guard against intrusion. Joseph Campbell noted that "in India…the 'serpent kings' guard both the waters of immortality and the treasures of the earth." [62]

While many male anthropologist and archaeologist argue that the serpent is symbolic of fertility (as a phallic symbol), art historian Merlin Stone offers another view:

"[The serpent] appears to have been primarily revered as a female in the Near and Middle East and generally linked to wisdom and

---

[61] Mackenzie, Donald A. *Ancient Man in Britain*. London: Senate 1996, 188-189. A reprint of the 1922 edition published by Blackie & Son Limited, London.
[62] Campbell, Joseph. *Creative Mythology: The Masks of God Volume IV*. London: Secker & Warburg 1968, 120.

prophetic counsel rather than fertility and growth as is so often suggested."[63]

This statement is not entirely true. The god Ningišzida ("Lord of the Good Tree") was an important male deity in Mesopotamia. As an underworld god, he was guardian over demons and at least one Sumerian ruler regarded Ningišzida as his personal protector. While primarily a god of the underworld there is one myth ("Adapa at the gate of heaven") that has Ningišzida as one of the guardians at the gates of heaven. [64] "The symbol and beast of Ningišzida," according to Black and Green, "was the horned snake..." [65]

The snake and the serpent have been depicted as goddesses and gods, as holy beings to be worshipped, as dragons, as devils and as symbols of lust, greed and sin—and of death. In mythic lore, Zeus appears in snake form to mate with Persephone who thereafter gives birth to Dionysos, "the god who in Crete, it so happens, was synonymous with Zeus." [66] The serpent is "the emblem of all self-creative divinities and represents the generative power of the earth. It is solar, chthonic, sexual, funerary and the manifestation of force at any level, a source of all potentialities both material and spiritual," writes

---

[63] Stone, Merlin. *When God Was A Woman*. New York: Barnes & Noble Books 1993, 199.

[64] Black, Jeremy and Anthony Green. *Gods, Demons and Symbols of Ancient Mesopotamia*. Austin: University of Texas Press 2000, 139.

[65] Ibid 140.

[66] Baring, Anne and Jules Cashford. *The Myth of the Goddess: Evolution of an Image*. London: Arkana/Penguin Books 1991, 317.

J.C. Cooper, "and closely associated with the concepts of both life and death." [67]

The Giants of classic Greek and Roman mythology reportedly had snake-like legs as did the founder of Athens, Cecrops. Cecrops, a semi-serpent, was considered an innovator of his day, abolishing blood sacrifice, introducing basic laws of marriage, politics and property and encouraging the worship of Zeus and Athena. [68] Again, a duality exists between these two creatures with snake-like characteristics. The Giants were enemies of Zeus and were defeated by Hercules on behalf of the gods of Olympus, Cecrops became a champion for the causes of Zeus.

Zeus conquers the Serpent-legged Titans

Recent excavations in the Kenar Sandal area in Jiroft, Iran have uncovered additional serpent-legged figures. According to the *Persian*

[67] Cooper, J.C. *An Illustrated Encyclopaedia of Traditional Symbols*. London : Thames and Hudson 1978, 147.
[68] Cotterell, Arthur. *The Encyclopedia of Mythology: Classical, Celtic, Greek*. London: Hermes House 2005, 84.

Journal,[69] the reliefs depicting two men with "snake tails instead of legs" were carved on soapstone on a "flat stone cliff." At one time almost 5,000 years ago, Kenar Sandal was an important trade city for the Persian Gulf region, linking what is now present day Afghanistan, Pakistan, Iran and Tajikistan. The serpent-men reliefs indicate that this image has an ancient origin most likely outside the classic Greco-Roman world.

In support of the view that this mythic creature originated in the non-Classic World are the serpent-men of the Indian Underworld, the "demonic Cobras" called the Nagas. According to Mackenzie "they are of human form to the waist, the rest of their bodies being like those of serpents." [70] The Nagas were demi-gods to the Indian serpent worshippers and were, according to Mackenzie, "occasionally 'the friends of man', and to those they favoured they gave draughts of their nectar, which endowed them with great strength." [71]

Abrasax Gem Amulet

---

[69] "New Stone Reliefs Discovered in Jiroft, Iran" in *Persian Journal*, February 2, 2006. http://www.iranian.ws/iran_news/publish/article_12873.shtml
[70] Mackenzie, Donald A. *India Myths & Legends*. London: Studio Editions 1993, 65.
[71] Ibid., 66.

An interesting image similar to the serpent-legged Titans and the Nagas is that carved upon the strange "Abrasax gems", magical amulets introduced in the second century that mingled early Christian and Pagan themes. Originating in Alexandria, the images most certainly were inspired by the mystic powers of the man-serpent as represented by the Titans.

It is interesting to note that Athens has even more connections to serpent-men in the form of Erichthonius—the first king of Athens. According to legend, this serpent being was created from the semen of the smith-god Hephaistos. Hephaistos had attempted to rape Athena but she miraculously disappeared just in time. His semen, as it fell to the earth, grew into the serpent Erichthonius. Ely offers an alternative view: "In the days of Pausanias, Hephaistos and Gaia were said to be the parents of Erichthonius." This version evidently arose from the more conservative elements of Greek society that could not abide with the original creation of the serpent-being from an act of rape. [72]

In Mesoamerican traditions, the Plumed Serpent, Quetzalcoatl, called "the wise instructor," brings culture and knowledge to the people and "takes charge or interferes in creative activities" of the world. [73] It is Quetzalcoatl who discovers corn and provides it for humankind's nourishment. While historical lore indicates that

---

[72] Ely, Talfourd. *The Gods of Greece and Rome.* Mineola: Dover Publications Inc. 2003, 161. A reprint of the 1891 edition published by G.P. Putnam's Sons, New York.
[73] Bierhorst, John. *The Mythology of Mexico and Central America.* New York: William Morrow and Company 1990, 145.

Quetzalcoatl was a man (in fact, a tall, white man with a beard), he is symbolically represented as a serpent on many temple complexes, the most notable being at Chichen-Itza in Yucatan. During certain times of the year the steps the lead up the pyramid temple cast an undulating shadow that connects with the carved stone serpent heads—bringing to life the Plumed Serpent.

Quetzalcoatl atop a ruin at Chichen-Itza

The serpent also represents chaos, corruption and darkness along with knowledge and spirit. It is this knowledge that the Bible uses to evict Adam and Eve from paradise and what brings the snake so much hatred. It is the symbolism of the snake, that is so closely associated with the Earth and the Earth's creative powers that the followers of the Sky God wished to destroy. According to Andrews, the snake "threatened the world order established by the sky gods and continually tried to return the world to its original state of chaos."[74]

The serpent, in fact, threatened the order and control of the Judeo-Christian religion. As Markale suggests, Eve disobeyed the patriarchal priests and listens to the serpent, the serpent being representative of the Mother Goddess. "This is a case, pure and simple, of a return to the mother-goddess cult, a true 'apostasy' as it were, and thus a very grave sin against the patriarchal type of religion that Yahweh represents."[75] Markale and others, most notably the French Catholic priest André de Smet, believe that the original sin was the first battle in the long struggle between the patriarchal religion of Yahew and the matriarchal religion of the Mother Goddess. The "curse against the serpent," Markale writes, "...is against the mother goddess herself." [76]

The Gnostic writers viewed the serpent in a different manner. The Kabbalist Joseph Gikatila wrote in his book *Mystery of the Serpent*:

"Know and believe that the Serpent, at the beginning of creation, was indispensable to the order of the world, so long as he kept his place; and he was a great servent...and he was needed for the ordering of all the chariots, each in its place...It is he who moves the spheres and turns them from East to the West and from North to the South.

---

[74] Andrews, Tamra. *A Dictionary of Nature Myths*. Oxford: Oxford University Press 1998, 176.
[75] Markale, op cit, 6.
[76] Ibid, 7.

Without him there would have been neither seed nor germination, nor will to produce any created thing."[77]

The Ophites, a successor group of the original Gnostics, venerated the snake. To the Ophites the serpent was made by God to be "the cause of Gnosis for mankind...It was the serpent...who taught man and woman the complete knowledge of the mysteries on high" which resulted in the serpent being "cast down from the heavens." [78] To this group the snake was the "living symbol of the celestial image that they worshipped."[79] According to Doresse, the Ophites kept and fed serpents in special baskets and met near the serpent's burrows. They would arrange loaves of bread on a table and then lure the snakes to the "offering". The Ophite followers would not partake of the bread however until "each on kissing the muzzle of the reptile they had charmed. This, they claimed, was the perfect sacrifice, the true Eucharist."[80] To the Gnostic Christians, serpent worship was associated with the "restoration of Paradise, and release thereby from the bondages of time." [81]

A similar ritual has taken place each August 15th on the Greek island of Kefalonia. On this day, also known as the feast of the Falling Asleep of the Virgin, in the small village of Markopoulo, small snakes with a small cross-like mark on their heads slither through a

---

[77] As quoted by Jean Doresse, *The Secret Books of the Egyptian Gnostics*. New York: MJF Books 1986, 292-293.
[78] Ibid, 44.
[79] Ibid, 45.
[80] Ibid, 44.
[81] Campbell, op cit. 151.

churchyard, emerging near the bell tower and make their way toward the church. According to witnesses, the snakes enter the church building through bell rope holes in the wall; crawl over the furniture and even over the worshippers as they sit in the pews. The snakes continue onward to the bishop's throne and, as a group, to the icon of the Virgin.

After the service, the serpents disappear and not seen again until the same evening a year later. The people of Markopoulo look forward to the appearance of these creatures as a sign of good luck and bountiful harvests. Only two years in recent memory did not see the return of the snakes. One was in 1940. The next year Greece was invaded by the Axis Forces. The year following their non-appearance in 1953 saw the area devastated by a catastrophic earthquake.

Normally avoiding human contact during their visits to the church the snakes appear quite tame and allow the residents to handle them at will. According to local lore, the annual serpent appearance dates to 1705 when Barbarossa pirates attacked the village. The nuns who resided in the village convent prayed to the Virgin to transform them into snakes to avoid being captured by the pirates, or worse. When the pirates finally gained access to the convent, they were shocked to see the floors, walls and icons writhing with snakes. The snakes have returned each year except for the two previously mentioned.

The serpent, as a representative of the mother goddess, is known from the serpent priestesses of Crete and various other mother goddess locations from the Neolithic. The shrine at Gournia, Crete yielded three figures of the mother goddess. One that shows the mother goddess with a serpent curled around her waist and over one shoulder.[82] The Greek mother goddess Ge or Gaia is often associated with the "earth snake."

Twenty-one figurines of serpent goddesses have been found at Poduri, Romania dating to 4800-4600 BCE indicating that this goddess was not only an ancient one but commonly worshiped throughout Europe and the Middle East. Archaeologist Marija Gimbutas wrote "Their lack of arms, their snake-shaped heads, and the snakes coiling over their abdomens suggest that they represent the Snake Goddess and her attendants, only one of them has an arm raised to her face, a gesture of power." [83]

Similar goddesses were worshipped in ancient Knossos and were, according to James, "the principal objects of veneration in the public sanctuary, and in a small chamber known as the Snake Room of a private house" where carvings of snakes drinking from cups decorated the walls. [84]

The serpent has been associated with water since time began. "Undulating serpents or dragons signify cosmic rhythm, or the power of the waters." [85] They appear in Native American rock art throughout the continent symbolic of messengers of the otherworld that traverse

---

[82] Mackenzie, Donald A. *Myths and Legends Crete & Pre-Hellenic*. London: Senate 1995, 261. A reprint of the 1917 edition published as *Crete & Pre-Hellenic Europe* by The Gresham Publishing Company, London.
[83] Gimbutas, op cit, 343.
[84] James, E.O. *The Ancient Gods*. Edison: Castle Books 2004, 100.
[85] Cooper, op cit, 148.

through streams, rivers and time through the cracks in stone. It is by no accident that the Plumed Serpent of Mesoamerica is closely associated with the Cosmic Waters or that the Serpent Mound in the Ohio Valley is located near a flowing river. It is also not an accident that accounts of sea serpents are rampant in the world's maritime lore. In the Southwest, snakes were pecked or painted onto rock surfaces designating good or bad water sources. The snake was believed by Native Americans, as well as to the people of Old Europe and the ancient Near East, to bring rain when it is needed. Both the Hopi and Shasta Indians carried live snakes in their mouths for ritual dances used in rainmaking ceremonies[86] and the Cheyenne also danced with poisonous snakes in their "crazy dances". "Crazy dances" were performed to aid in the cure of a sick child, to ensure victory in war or to obtain other blessings for the tribe.[87]

Snakes have also contributed to weather folklore around the world associated with rain. Nineteenth century folklorist Richard Inwards noted, "the chief characteristic of the serpents throughout the East in all ages seems to have been their power over the wind and rain, which they gave or withheld, according to their good or ill will towards man."[88] It was also possible to induce rain, according to Inwards, by hanging a dead snake on a tree. [89]

---

[86] Kasner, Leone Letson. *Spirit Symbols in Native American Art*. Philomath: Ayers Mountain Press 1992, 113.

[87] Mooney, James. *The Ghost-Dance Religion and the Sioux Outbreak of 1890*. Chicago: The University of Chicago Press 1965, 273.

[88] Inwards, Richard. *Weather Lore*. London: Elliot Stock 1893.

[89] Ibid.

Mesoamerican traditions "have been recorded," writes anthropologist Robert Rands, "which directly connect the serpent with surface water, rain, and lightning. ...a few stray facts regarding the relationship of snakes to the anthropomorphic rain deities of the Maya and Mexicans may be noted. In the Maya codices, the serpent...and water are frequently shown together...As giant celestial snakes or as partly anthropomorphized serpents, the Chicchans are rain and thunder deities of the present-day Chorti. ...In modern Zoque belief, snakes serve as the whips of the thunderbolts." [90]

The snake with its fluid motions is a natural symbol of flowing water. Native Americans and others saw this symbolism in the meandering streams and rivers that flow through their lands. They also saw the annual shedding of its skin as a renewal of life and of fertility, a renewal of the fertility that water also provides.

"The serpent is the foundation of the universe," writes Indian artist Jyoti Sahi. "Coiled around the naval of the cosmos, it appears to be the dynamic centre of time and space. The serpent seems always to be moving and yet always still, like the oceans whose waves seem in perpetual turmoil and unrest, but whose boundaries remain fixed, and whose depths are eternal." [91]

---

[90] Rands, Robert L. "Some Manifestations of Water in Mesoamerican Art," Anthropological Papers, No. 48, Bureau of American Ethnology Bulletin 157. Washington: Smithsonian Institution 1955, 361, pgs 265-393.
[91] Sahi, Jyoti. The Child and the Serpent: Reflections on Popular Indian Symbols. London: Arkana/Penguin Books 1980, 161.

In ancient Indian mythology, the serpent becomes the victim of mankind, "…in order to overcome the wilderness…and make it orderly and cultivated…[man] had to injure the serpent…" [92] Sahi says that this injury to the serpent is a "sin" and that the story really "represents the overthrowing of pre-Aryan serpent worship." [93]

In the ancient Mesopotamian city of Ur, the snake god Irhan was worshipped. To these people Irhan was representative of the Euphrates River. The mildly poisonous horned vipers of the Middle East gradually assumed the dragon form that we still recognize today.

A snake-dragon called *mušhuššu*, or "furious snake" was worshipped in Babylon at least during the reign of Nebuchadnezzar II (604-562 BCE). This creature with the body and neck of a serpent, lion's forelegs and a bird's hindlegs, was originally an attendant of the city god Ninazu of Ešnunna. The snake-dragon was transferred as an attendant of Ninazu to several other national gods through the years, surviving as a protective pendant through the Hellenistic Period. [94]

The serpent was present in the liturgy and symbolism of the Mithraic religion as well. Mithraism almost dominated Christianity during the 2nd and 3rd centuries and many Christian symbols are derived from this ancient religion. The snake appears often in paintings and carvings of Mithras hunting, the serpent is present as a companion to the god. Some depict the serpent seeking the flowing sacrificial blood

---

[92] Ibid, 165.
[93] Ibid, 166.
[94] Jeremy and Anthony Green. *Gods, Demons and Symbols of Ancient Mesopotamia*. Austin: University of Texas Press 2000, 166.

of the bull that was slain in Mithraic baptisms. This, according to writer D. Jason Cooper, "seems to indicate the snake is seeking salvation."[95]

Snakes are also associated with healing. The caduceus, the staff with two intertwined serpents, is found not only in the healing temples of Greece, but also in Native American, Mesoamerican and Hindu symbolism. The snake with its annual shedding of its skin was a logical symbol for life, renewal and protection. In Celtic lands as well the snake was, like the sacred well, associated with healing. To the Sumerians the caduceus was the symbol of life. The caduceus was also an important symbol to some Gnostic Christians who, according to Barbara Walker, "worshipped the serpent hung on a cross...or Tree of Life, calling it Christ the Savior, also a title of Hermes the Wise Serpent represented by his own holy caduceus..." [96]

According to Wallis Budge, "the symbol of [the Bablyonian god of healing, Ningishzida] was a staff round which a double-sexed, two-headed serpent called Sachan was coiled, and a form of this is the recognized mark of the craft of the physician at the present day." [97] The Greek god of healing, Aesculapius was also depicted in a statue at

[95] Cooper, D. Jason. *Mithras: Mysteries and Initiation Rediscovered.* York Beach: Samuel Weiser, Inc. 1996, 74.
[96] Walker, Barbara G. *The Women's Encyclopedia of Myths and Secrets.* Edison: Castle Books 1996, 131.
[97] Budge, E.A. Wallis. *Babylonian Life and History.* New York: Barnes & Noble Books 2005, 167.

Epidaurus "holding a staff in one hand, while his other hand rested on the head of a snake..."[98]

In Africa the spirits of the waters are, simply said, snakes. As they are symbolic of healing, they are also believed to "call" to healers to whom they give wisdom and knowledge.[99] According to anthropologist Penny Bernard, "the water spirits have been attributed a pivotal role in the calling, initiation and final induction of certain diviners in the Eastern Cape. Hence the implication that they are the key to certain forms of 'sacred' knowledge."[100]

Tornadoes and waterspouts were believed to be the physical appearance of the African serpent god Inkanyamba. Inkanyamba was believed to be an enormous serpent that twisted and writhed to and fro as it reached from the earth to the sky. Tamra Andrews noted that the Zulu "believed that he grew larger and larger as he rose out of his pool and then grew smaller and smaller when he retreated back into it."[101]

In other African cultures, the snake is considered the spirit of a departed human. Referred to as the 'living-dead' the snake is prohibited from being killed, as it is representative of the soul of a relative or friend that is visiting the land of the living.[102]

---

[98] Ibid.
[99] Bernard, Penny. "Mermaids, Snakes and the Spirits of the Water in Southern Africa: Implications for River Health", op cit., 3.
[100] Ibid., 4.
[101] Andrews, op cit, 96.
[102] Mbiti, John S. *African Religions and Philosophy*. Garden City: Anchor Books 1970, 216.

According to Sumatran and Norse mythology, the vast Cosmic Snake that encircles the world in the cosmic river will eventually destroy it. However from the destruction comes a new world, a renewal of life. The old gods die with the Cosmic Serpent but "Earth will rise again from the waves, fertile, green, and fair as never before, cleansed of all its sufferings and evil."[103]

Perhaps in no other culture than Egypt was the serpent-god so prevalent. In ancient Egypt, the snake represented the "Great God" whose powers extended from heaven to the earth. The serpent, however, represented both male and female deities, both benign and malevolent. The snake-god Apophis was believed to have existed before time in the primeval chaos of pre-creation. Apophis was the enemy of the sun god and attacked the heavenly ship of Ra as it sojourned across the heavens. The daily battle involved other gods, including Seth the enemy of Osiris, in a back and forth struggle of power between light and dark and balance and chaos. Each day Apophis was defeated, cut into pieces that would revive and rejoin the struggle the next day. In his own way Apophis was a symbol of renewal—renewal brought about by the eternal conflict of the powers of the universe. Apophis was associated with natural disaster, storms, earthquakes and unnatural darkness that foretold the return of chaos. As archaeologist Richard Wilkinson wrote, "Although the god was neither worshipped in a formal cult nor incorporated into popular

---

[103] Davidson, H. R. Ellis. *Gods and Myths of the Viking Age*. New York: Bell Publishing Company 1981, 38.

veneration, Apophis entered both spheres of religion as a god or demon to be protected against." [104]

The Egyptians worshiped ten other snake gods. These include Mehen who helped protect Ra from the daily attacks of Apophis, Denwen who was very much like a dragon and had the ability to cause a fiery conflagration, Kebehwet who was a "celestial serpent," Meretseger called the "goddess of the pyramidal peak" and who presided over the necropolis at Thebes. Meretseger became an important deity of the workers who constructed the burial temples and chambers and many representations of this serpent goddess have been found in workers' homes and shops in the area.

Other serpent gods of the Egyptians include Nehebu-Kau, "he who harnesses the spirits." [105] Nehebu-Kau was regarded as a helpful deity and was the son of the scorpion goddess Serket. He was referred to in hieroglyph as the "great serpent, multitudinous of coils" and was sometimes depicted as a man with a serpents head. Other beneficent serpent gods include Renenutet, a guardian of the king and goddess of the harvest and fertility. She was also known as a divine nurse. The cobra goddess Wadjet ("the green one") was a goddess of the Nile Delta and was associated with the world of the living rather than the world of the dead. Wadjet was another protector of the king and had

---

[104] Wilkinson, Richard H. *The Complete Gods and Goddesses of Ancient Egypt.* New York: Thames & Hudson 2003, 223.

[105] Ibid, 224.

the ability to spit flames as a defensive measure. The serpent on the pharaoh's crown was that of Wadjet. Like Renenutet, Wadjet was also a nurse to the god Hathor while he was yet a divine infant. Another fiery serpent is Wepset. Wepset, meaning "she who burns," guarded the king, other gods and the Eye of Ra. It was written in ancient texts that the Egyptian island of Biga was her cult center.

The last two Egyptian serpent deities are Weret-Hekau and Yam. "Great of magic" was the name for Weret-Hekau and she may be a composite of other serpent goddesses in that she was also a nursing serpent of the kings and her symbol is associated with the other uraeus goddesses. Yam was actually a Semitic god, a "tyrannical, monstrous deity of the sea", according to Wilkinson.[106] Sometimes depicted as a seven-headed sea monster, Yam was a minor Egyptian god that may have been feared mostly by sailors and fishermen than by regular people of the cities. Yam was defeated in various myths by the goddess Astarte, and the Canaanite god Baal and the Egyptian god Seth.

Serapis, a deity of both the Greeks and Egyptians, associated with Osiris, Hermes, and Hades, was introduced in the 3rd century BCE as a state god for both Greeks and Egyptians. Believed by the Egyptians to be a human manifestation of Apis, a sacred bull that symbolized Osiris, he was represented as a god of fertility and medicine and the ruler of the dead to the Greeks. Serapis was also depicted as a Sun god

---

[106] Ibid, 228.

and occasionally with a serpent wrapped around his body—most likely in connection with fertility.

Serapis

That serpents were, and still are an extremely important aspect of religious traditions around the world cannot be doubted when even Ireland, a land totally devoid of snakes, is so obsessed with the image of the serpent. "Is it not a singular circumstance," said 19th century scholar Marcus Keane, "that in Ireland where no living serpent exists, such numerous legends of serpents should abound, and that figures of serpents should be so profusely used to ornament Irish sculptures?" [107] Celtic scholar James Bonwick himself noted when he visited Cashel, Ireland in the 1880's that he saw "a remarkable stone, bearing a nearly defaced sculpture of a female—head and bust—but whose legs were snakes." [108] It was Bonwick's belief that this ancient stone carving

---

[107] As quoted by James Bonwick in *Irish Druids and Old Irish Religions*. New York: Barnes & Noble Books 1986, 173. A reprint of the 1894 edition.
[108] Ibid 174.

depicted an "object of former worship." The "popularity" of the serpent image in Ireland caused Bonwick to write, "That one of the ancient military symbols of Ireland should be a serpent, need not occasion surprise in us. The Druidical serpent or Ireland is perceived in the Tara brooch, popularize to the present day. Irish crosses, so to speak, were alive with serpents."[109]

Serpents were valued in Slavic countries up through the 19th century as good-luck symbols. Snakes were also valued as protective charms in Sweden where they were buried under the foundations of houses and other structures. Russian peasants kept them as pets and, as in Poland; snakes were given food and drink in exchange for their protective charms.

Snakes were associated with an ancient god of thunder in Slavic countries. The thunder god was "responsible for creating mountains and for hurling down bolts of lightning also launched storms of life-giving rain into the earth beneath him."[110] Kerrigan writes "Awesome as his strength was, pagan belief did not characterize it as being wielded destructively: only with the coming of Christianity did his powers become identified with those of evil."[111]

In some Native American lore, the snake was usually considered an animal to be avoided—one of the "bad animals" that was prohibited

---

[109] Ibid 168.
[110] Kerrigan, Michael. "A Fierce Menagerie" in *Forests of the Vampire: Slavic Myth.* New York: Barnes & Noble 2003, 124.
[111] Ibid.

from journeying to the spirit world after death. [112] To the Lakota the spirit of the snake "presided over the ability to do things slyly, to go about unknown and unseen, and of lying."[113]

Cherokee shamans prohibited the killing of snakes and the Apache forbid the killing of any snake by their own people but would not hesitate to ask strangers to kill them.[114] The Cherokee generic name for the snake is *inădû'* and they are believed to be supernatural, having close associations with rain and the thunder gods, as well as having a certain influence over other plants and animals. "The feeling toward snakes," wrote James Mooney, "is one of mingled fear and reverence, and every precaution is taken to avoid killing or offending one..."[115] Certain shamans were able to kill rattlesnakes for use in rituals or for medicinal uses. The head was always cut off and buried an arms length deep in the earth. If this was not done, the snake would cause the rain to fall until the streams and rivers overflowed their banks. [116]

Specific snake lore of the Cherokee indicates that some serpents were not only associated with rain, thunder and the supernatural but also were very unlucky. Mooney reported that a large serpent was once

---

[112] Walker, James R. *Lakota Belief and Ritual.* Lincoln: University of Nebraska Press 1991, 71.

[113] Ibid, 122.

[114] Bourke, John G. *Apache Medicine-Men.* New York: Dover Publications, Inc. 1993, 20. A reprint of the1892 edition of *The Medicine-Men of the Apache* published in the Ninth Annual Report of the Bureau of Ethnology to the Secretary of the Smithsonian Institution 1887-88, Washington, pgs 443-603.

[115] Mooney, James. *Myths of the Cherokee.* New York: Dover Publications 1995, 294.

[116] Ibid, 296.

said to reside on the north bank of the Little Tennessee and the main Tennessee rivers in Loudon county, Tennessee and it was considered an evil omen simply to see it. "On one occasion," he wrote, "a man crossing the river…saw the snake in the water and soon afterward lost one of his children." [117]

Illnesses were often thought to be caused by snakes, and even the act of accidentally touching the discarded skin of a snake was believed to cause sickness, especially skin ailments and perhaps even death. [118]

The Apache avoided even mentioning the snake but would sometimes use it as an invective. However, by doing even this one courted disaster. According to Opler, "If a man says in anger, 'I hope a snake bites you,' he will get sick from snakes. ..Before this the snakes have not bothered him, but…it's bound to make him sick." [119]

When a snake is accidentally encountered on a trail, it is, according to Opler, "accorded the greatest respect and is referred to by a relationship term: …"My mother's father, don't bother me! I'm a poor man. Go where I can't see you. Keep out of my path." [120]

Cherokee lore tells of strange snake-like creatures that were obviously more than myth as no tale of heroes or supernatural interventions are part of the tales. They are simply told as observations

---

[117] Mooney, op cit 414.
[118] Opler, Morris Edward. *An Apache Life-Way: The Economic, Social, and Religious Institutions of the Chiricahua Indians.* Chicago: The University of Chicago Press 1941, 228.
[119] Ibid.
[120] Ibid, 227.

and accounts of frightful encounters between men and monster. One such beast is called the Ustû'tlĭ, or "foot snake" which lived on the Cohutta Mountain. Ethnologist James Mooney recorded stories at the beginning of the 20th century about this monster and gives us the following description:

"…it did not glide like other snakes, but had feet at each end of its body, and moved by strides or jerks, like a great measuring worm. These feet were three-cornered and flat and could hold on to the ground like suckers. It had no legs, but would raise itself up on its hind feet, with its snaky head waving high in the air until it found a good place to take a fresh hold…It could cross rivers and deep ravines by throwing its head across and getting a grip with its front feet and then swinging it body over." [121]

A similar creature called the "bouncer" (Uw'tsûñ'ta) lived on the Nantahala River in North Carolina. It too moved by "jerks like a measuring worm." According to lore this snake like animal was so immense that it would darken the valleys between rifts as it moved across them. According to Mooney the Indians that lived in this area, fearing the snake eventually deserted the land, "even while still Indian country." [122]

Another monstrous snake, called the Uktena, was said to be as large as a tree trunk with horns on its head. To be able to kill the

---

[121] Mooney, op cit 1995, 302.

[122] Ibid, 304.

Uktena enabled the Uktena slayer to obtain a transparent scale from the snake, said to be similar to a crystal that was located on its forehead. To have one was to be blessed with excellent hunting, success in love, rainmaking and life prophecy.

Some Native American people viewed the snake in another way entirely. It was symbolic of the war-god who also had powers over crops and vegetation. "As the emblem of the fertilizing summer showers the lightning serpent was the god of fruitfulness," wrote Lewis Spence, "but as the forerunner of floods and disastrous rains it was feared and dreaded." [123]

That pre-historic Indians believed that the serpent form contained supernatural powers can be surmised by the various serpent mounds constructed in the American heartland. Three such mounds are those found in Adams County, Ohio, St. Peter's River, Iowa and another serpentine mound which extends in sections over two miles in length, also in Iowa. The Great Serpent Mound located in Adams County, Ohio is believed to be the largest serpent effigy in the world at over one-quarter of a mile in length and depicts a serpent in the act of uncoiling. [124] This unusual earthwork shows the serpent with an egg, perhaps the Cosmic Egg, in its mouth. The culture that created the Great Serpent Mound is unknown since no manmade artifact has been

---

[123] Spence, Lewis. *North American Indians Myths & Legends*. London: Senate 1994, 112. A reprint of *North American Indians* published 1914 by George G. Harrap & Company Ltd.

[124] Silverberg, Robert. *Mound Builders of Ancient America: The Archaeology of a Myth*. Greenwich: New York Graphic Society Ltd. 1968, 249.

found in connection with the site, although Adena artifacts consisting of copper breastplates, stone points and axes, and grooved sandstone have been found within 400 feet of the mound.

Depictions of snakes holding the Cosmic Egg were important figures in Native American petroglyphs as shown in the photograph below.

South West American Indian petroglyph of the snake with the cosmic egg

A serpent mound similar to the one located in Ohio and dated to the Bronze Age was discovered in Herefordshire, England during the excavation of a new roadway. Mounds of "burned stone" were intentionally arranged in the form of a giant serpent 65-yards in length (195 feet). Nearby burials and burned timbers added to the ritual significance of the site. The Herefordhsire serpent mound is at least

3,000 years older than the mound in Ohio but their functions may very well have been identical and they certainly represent a divine nature. [125]

British folklore says, "if you wear a snake skin round your head, you will never have a headache" and "snakes never die until the sun goes down, however much they may be cut in pieces." [126] However, "if you kill one its mate will come looking for you." [127]Another advises that to stay young—eat snake!

In 19th century Gaelic folklore the serpent is more evil than good. Campbell wrote, "A serpent, whenever encountered, ought to be killed. Otherwise, the encounter will prove an evil omen.

"The head should be completely smashed…and removed to a distance from the rest of the body. Unless this is done the serpent will again come alive. The tail, unless deprived of animation, will join the body, and the head becomes a *beithir,* the largest and most deadly kind of serpent." [128]

In other cultures, like those of Native America, there is a prohibition against killing snakes. Frazer wrote "In Madras it is considered a great sin to kill a cobra. When this has happened, the people generally burn the body of the serpent, just as they burn the bodies of human beings. The murderer deems himself polluted for

---

[125] "Unique Bronze Age serpentine mound found in Western England" in *International Herald Tribune*, July 4, 2007.
[126] Radford, Edwin and Mona A. *Encyclopaedia of Superstitions*. New York: Philosophical Library 1949, 221.
[127] Simpson, Jacqueline and Steve Roud. *Oxford Dictionary of English Folklore*. Oxford: Oxford University Press 2000, 2.
[128] Campbell, John Gregorson. *The Gaelic Otherworld,* edited by Ronald Black. Edinburgh: Birlinn Limited 2005, 121.

three days."[129] In other areas of the world, snakes were annually sacrificed in large numbers by burning. This occurred at Luchon in the Pyrenees on Midsummer Eve at least into the early 20th century. Considered a Pagan survival, the ritual was led by the local clergy. Frazer describes the event:

"At an appointed hour—about 8 PM—a grand procession, composed of the clergy, followed by young men and maidens in holiday attire, pour forth from the town chanting hymns, and take up their position [around a wicker-work column raised 60 feet in height]. ...bonfires are lit, with beautiful effect, in the surrounding hills. As many living serpents as could be collected are now thrown into the column, which is set on fire at the base by means of torches, armed with which about fifty boys and men dance around with frantic gestures. The serpents...wriggle their way to the top...until finally obliged to drop, their struggles for life giving rise to enthusiastic delight among the surrounding spectators." [130]

Serpents have been mercilessly hunted and killed by many cultures the world over but it is possible, according to Jyoti Sahi, that "all religions which have evolved the concept of a really personal god...have emerged out of a tradition in which serpents have been extremely important symbols of the supernatural." [131]

---

[129] Frazer, Sir James. *The Golden Bough: A study in magic and religion.* Hertfordshire: Wordsworth Editions 1993, 222.
[130] Ibid 655-656.
[131] Sahi, op cit 166.

Perhaps the oldest example of human ritual has recently been discovered [132] in a remote cave in the Kalahari Desert of Botswana. Some 70,000 years ago, in an area known as the "Mountains of the Gods," a group of people carved a huge python from the natural stone. Taller than a man and twenty feet long, the artificial serpent was crafted in such a way to make the skin look natural as the sunlight plays over the form—also making it appear to move.

Near the serpent archaeologists found several burned spearpoints that had been brought to the cave from several hundred miles away. The burned aspect of the spearpoints indicates that they had been used in a religious ritual.

The modern tribes people, the San, have an ancient legend that mankind descended from the python. Obviously the ancient sculpture has been an important part of the culture and religion of the people living in this area for thousands of years.

The Horned Snake

Snakes with horns? They are common in Celtic artistic mythology and represent protection against all forms of catastrophe—sickness, war and all of the horrors of death. According to Miranda Green, approximately fifteen examples of horned serpents can be found in Gaul while only a handful more are seen throughout the British Isles. [133]

---

[132] Britt, Robert Roy. "Startling Discovery: The First Human Ritual" http://www.livescience.com/history/061130_oldest_ritual.html November 30, 2006
[133] Green, Miranda. *The Gods of the Celts*. Gloucester: Alan Sutton 1986, 192.

The ram horned serpent almost always appears as a companion to Celtic deities such as Cernunnos, who himself is stag-horned. This monstrous snake appears on the Gundestrup Cauldron on one panel with Cernunnos and on another at the head of a military march. Miranda Green noted that the ram horned snake appears on a carving at Haute Marne accompanying a goddess who feeds the snake from a basket on her knee and at Loire on a wooden sculpture with a possible Cernunnos figure. The serpent slides down the god's arm with its head in a basket. "The repeated prosperity-symbolism," Green writes "shown in reliefs is significant: a bronze from…Seine et Loire combines several Celtic images in curious intensity; a three-headed god sits cross-legged…[with] a ram-horned snake entwined round his body."[134]

The horned snake was also an important religious image in other areas of the world. As noted previously, the Mesopotamian god Ningišzida was depicted as a horned snake, appearing on such items as ritual cups and city seals. Images of horned snakes were commonly used in the Mesopotamian world as magically protective charms.

While the snake was an extremely important deity in pre-Christian times, representing life, renewal, light and sacred mystery, it was denigrated by the dominating Christian religion, reduced to "the

---

[134] Ibid.

seducer, the tempter, the deceiver, and the very incarnation of the Spirit of Evil." [135]

[135] Charbonneau-Lassay, Louis. *The Bestiary of Christ.* New York: Arkana/Penguin Books 1992, 157.

Chapter Three
Gods of Nature

W ater sprites, Fairies, Bacchus, Pan and Dionysus are all gods and supernatural beings closely associated with nature. They represent the spirits of all— including plants, animals, stones, trees, the winds and all other aspects of this "natural" world and Otherworld. Earlier cultures expressed their traditions and beliefs orally in mythic form. Modern day society regards these myths as tales of fantasy and, even though some of them undoubtedly were the basis for Judeo-Christian lore, they are relegated to a "primitive" and "fairy tale" category. Simply said this is incorrect and ethnocentric. The dominant culture or leadership always discredits the traditions of others. As scholar John Bierhorst said, "myths are what others have; we ourselves have 'scripture' or 'history'." [136] These "myths" are as solid in their facts and meanings as the Biblical versions of history and they should not be denigrated. These early stories are the basis for modern day religious constructions and there is little difference between these myths and other "scriptures" than the change in the names of the heroes and gods. Myths were used to transmit actual events to non-literate cultures and were important for the way that they preserved these events generation to generation.

---

[136] Bierhorst, John. *The Mythology of Mexico and Central America.* New York: William Morrow and Company, Inc. 1990, 1

The contemporary and dominate religions of today regard animism as a primitive form of ancestral worship, worth little more than a footnote in the history of religion. Religious historians and scholars, such as Fred Skinner, take the view that "primitive people, ancient or modern, make no distinction between the natural and the supernatural...They have no knowledge of natural laws or natural causation. Speculation among the ancients could not take an intellectual or rational form; it had to be poetic or imaginative." [137]

I disagree with this analysis. To possess "knowledge of natural laws or causation" does not take away from the feelings of awe that anyone has of the forces of nature, the "behind-the-scenes" forces that cause massive storms or earthquakes or volcanoes. It does not matter that a scientist can "explain" why something happens; the event is still caused by forces beyond the scope of the average persons understanding or control. Much of our scientific theory used today was also known thousands of years ago—known by those same people who worshipped the Old Gods and recognized the spirits of nature. To know that something exists or happens *"because"* of certain forces does not displace the wonder felt toward these forces—nor should it. Nor do those explanations detract from the truly supernatural occurrences outside of scientific theory.

---

[137] Skinner, Fred Gladstone. *Myths and Legends of the Ancient Near East.* New York: Barnes and Noble Books 1970, 8

The dominant theory that "cults" are simply less than a true religion is a continuation of that ethnocentric mind-set dating to the early Christian era. At one time, the Eleusinian Mysteries dominated religion in the Mediterranean. For over 2000 years the Mystery Rites of Dionysus inspired philosophers, scholars and ordinary people from Egypt, Rome, Greece and other Mediterranean countries until the early Christian church ruled it a "cult" and set out to destroy it. Likewise, the followers of Mithra met with the same fate. Today we know that Mithraism was the basis for much of the Christian faith. Mithra had twelve followers, sat at a last supper, performed baptisms (in bulls blood) and was resurrected from the dead—promising eternal life. Constantine too declared it a "cult", just in time to prevent it from becoming the dominant religion, almost surpassing the new religion of Christianity.

Some scholars are blatant in their ethnocentrism and Judeo-Christian biases. Harvard anthropologist William Howells wrote, "it is quite true that we know their gods do not exist and their magic is hollow...". [138] What is missing in this assumption is that no one can prove if any god or gods exist, nor is it the right of anyone to say that they do not exist for a particular individual or group of people. The dominant religion normally espouses the view that only their religion is the true one and that the proof rests in some ancient record. Unfortunately, these ancient records are normally compiled from the

---

[138] Howells, William. *The Heathens: Primitive Man and His Religions.* Garden City: Anchor Books 1962, 6

lore and mythology of older religions, which had suffered conquest and, at times, annihilation at the hands of an invading and dominant religion and culture.

The annihilation of the Goddess centered, and the life espousing nature- oriented cultures came at the hands of nomadic warrior societies that replaced the Earth Goddess traditions with those of a patriarchal form. The goddess created life from within (the Earth). In a profound move the warrior societies replaced the Earth Goddess with a Sky God that created life from without (heaven)—this was the impetus that changed humankind's perceptions and relationships with nature. These nomads not only dealt physical devastation but also cultural impoverishment. [139] "Now everywhere", wrote Riane Eisler, "the men with the greatest power to destroy—the physically strongest, most insensitive, most brutal—rise to the top, as everywhere the social structure becomes more hierarchic and authoritarian. Women—who as a group...are most closely identified with the old view of power symbolized by the life-giving and sustaining chalice—are now gradually reduced to the status they are to hold hereafter: male-controlled technologies of production and reproduction.

"At the same time the Goddess herself gradually becomes merely the wife or consort of male deities, who...are now supreme." [140]

---

[139] Eisler, Riane. *The Chalice & The Blade: Our History, Our Future.* San Francisco: HarperSanFrancisco 1987, 52

[140] Ibid, 53

Nature has become the enemy of man to be used and abused—not nurtured and respected. The ancient Hebrews continued this attack as they entered the "Land of Milk and Honey". Not simply shepherds, the Hebrews did not just wander into a vacant paradise but took it by force from the Canaanites, killing all living things, including plant, animal, man, woman and child. The Canaanites were followers of the Goddess Asherah, also known as the Queen of Heaven, and many of the Hebrews also worshipped her. Over time, the Hebrew priest-class could not abide with a Goddess, even though the Goddess and the Hebrew Yahweh were worshipped side by side for hundreds of years. Those who refused to convert to the pure patriarchal-god system were slaughtered. [141]

The old myths were rewritten, as is done by all victors, to reflect the values of the dominate hierarchy—in this instance a male dominate society. References to the Goddess were stricken from religious texts, modified, or accidentally and unexplainably left intact. These mistakes have added a great deal of confusion to the religious teachings of the Jewish and Christian theologies for centuries.

The Gods of Nature, even though they are still with us, have been relegated to cartoon status because of the continued, albeit subconscious, rewriting of history and ridicule of the Old Religion.

---

[141] Patai, Raphael. *The Hebrew Goddess.* New York: Avon Books 1978. See Joshua 10:40: "So Joshua smote all the country of the hills, and of the south, and of the vale, and of the springs, and all their kings: he left none remaining, but utterly destroyed all that breathed...".

Perhaps the most successful mind control in history has been accomplished by the male dominated religions over the centuries. Control accentuated by torture, murder, slavery and cultural subjugation. However, you cannot keep a good idea down! The nature gods continue to rear their heads in the subtlest way. Christian churches were adorned with images of nature spirits; new mythologies grew out of the old and were added to the cultural library. These mythologies created links to the Old Religion and still survive as folklore. Contemporary fantasy writers such as Charles De Lint and Robert Holdstock continue to add to these mythologies and keep them alive—mixing ancient themes in a contemporary setting.

The Green Man image is found worldwide in contemporary jewelry and "garden décor". The Fairy can be found in every gift shop and their popularity only continues to grow. What is happening? Because the Old Religion has been part of the world and the human spirit since the beginning, it continues to resurface and to insinuate its creeping vines of influence into the human existence—to keep the message flowing that only with the cooperation, respect and love of humans towards nature can any of us survive.

"God" in the earliest time was known as gods of vegetation, the woodlands and renewal-resurrection. Some of these are Osiris, Attis, Adonis, Pan and Dionysus—and for our present work—the goddess Asherah.

All savior-gods, including Jesus, have a common theme. The story of Jesus, states David Leeming, "is a full blossoming...of the dying god myth…The 'pagan' sexual elements are gone, the planted seed and the resurrection of the savior king-god results for his followers not so much in the vegetation of spring (though this is a constant Easter theme in ritual if not in myth) as in a spiritual renewal…"[142] The common theme expressed is not only of the renewal of life, but also the renewal of the spirit. Many Christian writers try to show a major difference between the "Pagan" gods and Jesus, saying, "although imbued with special powers, they were nevertheless subject to fate. They did, in fact, die." [143] Nevertheless, like Jesus, they were also resurrected, promising a life after death to those who lived their lives in balance. Leeming points out that in the story of Jesus, "ultimately, immortality is celebrated in this story and in its ritual as it is in the other dying-god tales and ceremonies." [144]

Was Jesus another savior-god, a dying king, in a long string of gods promising renewal and resurrection linked intimately with the earth and vegetation? According to Sufi writer, Shawkat M. Toorawa the answer is yes. Khidr, the Green One, and Jesus, according to Toorawa, "have a profound connection with vegetation". [145] We may speculate that Paul and the other founders of Christianity manipulated the image

---

[142] Leeming, David Adams. *The World of Myth*. New York: Oxford University Press 1990, 157

[143] Carmichael, Joel. *The Birth of Christianity: Reality and Myth*. New York: Dorset Press 1989, 89

[144] Leeming, op cit

[145] Toorawa, Shawkat M. "Khidr: The History of a Ubiquitous Master" in *Sufi Selected Article*, Issue Number 30, Published by Khaniqahi Mimatullahi Publications 2000

of Jesus and the many religions of the day to incorporate all of the vital parts into one form that survived the first three centuries, ultimately dominating the Mediterranean world. Christianity, writes Carmichael, "had absorbed and digested all the essential rites, the fertile ideas, metaphors, and symbols with which pagan religions were themselves pullulating." [146]

The most important savior-gods, Adonis, Attis, Osiris, Dionysus, and Jesus met violent and untimely deaths, were "mourned by a loving goddess and annually celebrated by…worshippers." [147]

Osiris: Egyptian God of Vegetation, Death & Rebirth

When we think of the religious beliefs of the ancient Egyptians we normally see in our minds eye a plethora of gods and goddesses in a variety of shapes—both human and human-animal composites, and beasts of strange and frightening demeanor. In reality, there were only two gods that were important to the Egyptian people: Rā, the Sun god, and Osiris, the god of vegetation, death and resurrection. The Egyptians believed that Osiris was, according to Sir Wallis Budge, "of divine origin, that he suffered death and mutilation at the hands of the powers of evil, that after a great struggle with these powers he rose again, that he became henceforth the king of the underworld and the judge of the dead, and that because he had conquered death the

---

[146] Carmichael op cit 14.
[147] Spence. Lewis. *Ancient Egyptian Myths and Legends.* New York: Dover Publications, Inc. 1990, 71

righteous also might conquer death…" [148] At the birth of Osiris, the Greek writer Plutarch wrote in the 1st century CE, "a voice was heard, saying, 'The lord of all the earth is born.'" [149] While it is not my intent here to focus on the similarities between the Christian views of God or Jesus to Rā and Osiris, it is very interesting that the ancient Egyptians had similar views of their gods. As Budge noted, "He who was the son of Rā became the equal of his father, and he took his place side by side with him in heaven." [150]

Osiris, to the Egyptians, was regarded as a Tree Spirit—a true god of nature as the Tree Spirit watched over the crops, made them fertile, and guarded them from all forces of evil and blight until they were able to grow to maturity. In Egyptian myth, the dead Osiris was enclosed in a tree—much as Merlin, thousands of years later in the Arthurian mythos, was encased in one. It was not a coffin however as the tree is self-renewing, it survives the death of winter and blossoms once again in greenery in the spring. The tree became an important aspect of Osiris' worship, as it did to the followers of Baldar, Attis and Jesus. Each town and fishing village celebrated Osiris and erected a pillar, representative of the tree, in his honor. Originally, the pillar was simply a tree stripped of its branches but later this pillar became one of the hallmarks of Egyptian architecture. Egyptian inscriptions frequently

---

[148] Budge, Sir Wallis. *Egyptian Religion.* New York: Bell Publishing Company 1959, 61
[149] Ibid, 63
[150] Ibid, 83

refer to Osiris as residing in trees and Nut, his mother, is often depicted as a sycamore tree.

Osiris was perhaps the most widely worshipped god of Egypt and was the ultimate nature god. According to Tamra Andrews, Osiris was "a sky god because he maintained cosmic order, an earth god because he guaranteed fecundity of the soil, and a god of waters because his physical resurrection coincided with the annual resurrection of the Nile." [151] Burkert wrote in his book, *Ancient Mystery Cults*, "authentic Egyptian tradition has linked Osiris to the Nile, the life-giving water that dwindles away and yet comes back with the flood in summer." [152]

The origin of Osiris is lost in history. Mythology states that Osiris was a human king who became a god. His Egyptian name, as depicted in hieroglyphics, was the "Eye of Ra" but even ancient Egyptian texts were vague at best as to his perceived origin. Osiris is perhaps one of the oldest surviving nature gods of the world. Osiris, in Egyptian art, was colored either black to represent death, or green, like the Green Man, to represent his ties to vegetation.

Osiris, Isis and Horus, their son, were perhaps the first holy family—the first triad of religion. The holy family was significant in their influence on the Greco-Roman mystery religions and may have been significant in Christian mythology.

---

[151] Andrews, Tamra. *A Dictionary of Nature Myths: Legends of the Earth, Sea, and Sky*. Oxford: Oxford University Press 1998, 146
[152] Burkert, Walter. *Ancient Mystery Cults*. Cambridge: Harvard University Press 1987, 82

Even though Osiris was resurrected from the dead, he never really left the land of the dead instead, he became its ruler. Some scholars believe that this does not constitute true resurrection, as he did not rejoin the land of the living. This appears to be an insignificant distinction to me. If Jesus rose up and went to heaven, did he not stay with the dead? Osiris judged the dead, as does Jesus. Neither is different from the other in this regard.

Osiris was much more than ruler of the dead however. He was said to have given humankind the knowledge of agriculture and civilization, symbolizing the creative and fertile forces of nature and the renewing force of life.

Serapis

Serapis is another Egyptian god of fertility, renewal and rebirth. He is actually a composite god, a hybrid of several Greek and Egyptian deities. The Cult of Serapis had existed prior to the Ptolemaic Period but it was during this time that the influences of the Hellenistic deities affected this minor Egyptian cult. Originally a hybrid of Osiris and Apis,[153] Serapis was further transformed by the addition of characteristics of Zeus, Dionysus, Asklepius, Helios and Hades. He was the god of the sun, healing, fertility and the afterlife.

According to Wilkinson, Serapis "was portrayed in anthropomorphic form as a man wearing a Greek-style robe with

---

[153] Apis was the most important of the Egyptian bull deities, born of a virgin cow and the god Ptah. Apis was said to thresh the grain in the afterlife. He was an ancient god, worshipped at least in the 1st Dynasty (2920-2770 BCE).

Greek hairstyle and full beard and usually bearing a tall corn modius or measure on his head."[154] He is also depicted at times wearing ram's horns, as many of the Green Man images do up to the present day.

His main center of worship was in the Serapeum Temple in Alexandria, however evidence of smaller shrines and temples have been found as far away as York, England. A carved head of Serapis has also been found in London. Obviously, like the Green Man, Roman soldiers, traders and pilgrims were responsible for spreading the cult of Serapis throughout the Roman Empire.

Dionysus

Dionysus, god of the vine, drink and revelry. Rather innocuous items until you realize how important he was at one time in history. Dionysus, however, also was known for his healing powers obtained by devotees through their ecstatic rituals. Plato, writing in his *Phaedrus*, noted that these rituals were performed as a cure "for diseases and the greatest sufferings which manifest themselves in certain families, on account of some ancient cause or wrath." [155]

Dionysus, according to Ely, "was perhaps worshipped in Greece before men had learnt the art of cultivating the vine" not as a vegetation god but as "the powerful creator of the spring". [156] Like Osiris, Dionysus was associated with the life giving water, water that

---

[154] Wilkinson, Richarrd H. *The Complete Gods and Goddesses of Ancient Egypt.* London: Thames and Hudson 2003, 128

[155] Ibid 19

[156] Ely, Talfourd. *The Gods of Greece and Rome*. Mineola: Dover Publications Inc. 2003, 212. (A reprint of the 1891 edition published by G.P. Putnam's Sons)

provides renewal and regeneration. It was reported by Euripides that the followers of Dionysus were able to strike the earth with their wands and "at once" draw forth water. [157] Originally, Dionysus was regarded as the curator of nature, the powerful force of the fertility of the earth. In mythology, the Dryads, nymphs who lived in oak trees, were companions of Dionysus. As other gods became more important, he was relegated to being only the god of the vine. "The Dionysian myth, personifying nature's cycle of death and renewed life", wrote O'Grady, "…became a cult with wild and terrifying rites". [158] These rites became so well known that they "became the pattern for later conceptions of witches' Sabbaths." [159]

Many scholars believe that Dionysus and Pan were one and the same, but as people changed and viewed nature differently, Dionysus reflected those changes.

Is Dionysus reflected in those foliate masks that came to be known as Green Men? Most assuredly. Nineteenth-century folklorist J. H. Philpot wrote of an ancient symbol incorporating a tree "dressed as Dionysus". According to Philpot, "…a mask is fastened at the top of the trunk in such a way that the branches appear to grow from the

---

[157] Ibid, 213
[158] O'Grady, Joan. *The Prince of Darkness: The Devil in History, Religion and the Human Psyche*. New York: Barnes and Noble Books 1989, 45
[159] Ibid

head of the god, and the trunk is clothed with a long garment; a table, or altar, loaded with gifts stands beside it." [160]

Green Man researcher Ronald Millar noted as well that Dionysus was "always depicted with leafy beard and branches growing out of his head, symbolic of his role of god of trees in general." [161] Dionysus' popularity in Britain was probably more pronounced among the Roman occupiers than with the common folk. Near Glastonbury, a temple of Dionysus once existed but for the most part the horned god Cernunnos was already too well established among the Celts to be replaced by this foreign deity. However, the pervasive influence of Dionysus in Celtic-Romano culture cannot be underestimated. The spread of the Green Man motif can be directly tied to the march of the Roman army and, as odd as it may seem, with the spread of the Catholic Church which had included so many of the Pagan relics, myths and symbols of the religious traditions that the Church tried to suppress. Pagan survivals were well documented during the 14th century when a priory of monks in Devonshire was discovered to have been worshipping at a statue of Diana in a sacred grove.[162]

---

[160] Philpot, Mrs. J. H. *The Sacred Tree in Religion and Myth*. Mineola: Dover Publications Inc. 2004, 31 (A reprint of the 1897 edition published by Macmillan and Co. Ltd, New York & London)
[161] Millar, Ronald. *The Green Man Companion and Gazetteer*. East Sussex: S.B. Publications 1997, 11
[162] Ash, Steve. "Bacchus and Isis in Britain: Romano-British Mysteries and their descendants. A cultural, social, spiritual, political and psychological multiple perspective." www.angelfire.com/aka/Forum/BI ONE.htm July 11,2004

The Great God Pan: God of the Pasture and Country Life

Pan, the goat footed, horned player of the pipes is much more than the Disney cartoon figure romping through the daisy covered fields of Greece. To the herdsmen of ancient Greece he was the guardian of the flocks and to the Greek soldiers he was the "All-god". He caused such terror in the hearts of the Persians, enemies of Athens, that his actions are still common in today's languages as causing "panic". It is undoubtedly the image of Pan that the Christians took as their model for their personification of evil—Satan. [163] "It was not surprising that Pan," wrote Joan O'Grady, "the most earthy of all gods, should seem to be the nearest personification of the Prince of Darkness." [164] "As a god of nature," O'Grady continues, "he possessed powers of inspiration and prophecy. But especially he represented sexual desire, the force of destruction and creation. In Christian eyes, he became connected with everything that was evil."[165] When the early Christian Church was struggling to define the image of the force of evil (Satan), Pan's image fit their requirements perfectly. Regardless how future generations viewed Pan, he was, according to Servius, "formed in the likeness of Nature, inasmuch as he had horns to resemble the rays of the sun and the horns of the moon; that his face was ruddy in imitation of the ether; that he wore a spotted fawn-skin resembling the stars in

---

[163] Ely, op cit
[164] O'Grady, op cit 45
[165] O'Grady, op cit., 45

the sky; that his lower limbs were hairy because of trees and wild beasts; that he had feet resembling those of the goat to show the stability of the earth; that his pipe had seven reeds in accordance with the harmony of Heaven…that his pastoral staff bore a crook in reference to the year which curves back on itself; and, finally, that he was the God of all Nature." [166]

Pan was the God and protector of the wild creatures; he was also, under a different name, one of the eight ancient and original gods of Egypt—the earliest gods of the myriad to come. "Herodotus", writes Lewis Spence, "states that the god Pan and another goat-like deity were worshipped with a wealth of symbolic display and gorgeous rite as gods of generation and fecundity." [167]

As noted, the god Pan had origins in ancient history and was almost a universal deity. Perhaps the oldest god of the Greeks, Pan, king of the Arcadian satyrs, was also a consort to the Great Goddess, like the other young male sacrificial natures gods. To the Greeks the supreme Egyptian god, Amon-Ra, was the Egyptian representation of Pan. The Greeks even referred to Amon-Ra's Egyptian holy city as "Panopolis"—the City of Pan. Barbara Walker theorizes, "Pan's legend began with the Hindu fertility god Pancika, consort of one of the primal Mother-goddesses, many-breasted Hariti…" [168] While the god's

[166] Porteous, Alexander. *The Lore of the Forest: Myths and Legends*. London: Senate 1996, 117-118
[167] Spence, op cit, 288
[168] Walker, Barbara G. *The Women's Encyclopedia of Myths and Secrets*. Edison: Castle Books 1996, 765

origins are uncertain, we can be certain that he was perhaps the most important male deity in the ancient world. Pan was so important that his image became the Christian representation of Satan from the earliest days of the church. This image of the devil still survives into contemporary culture. This intentional act to "demonize" the gods of a people, so that another religion may be substituted, has been used for thousands of years and continues to this day.

16th century depiction of Satan (in the form of Pan) with St. Jerome

Pan had begun as a god of the wood; in fact, one of his titles was "Lord of the Woods". Over time, his attributes grew to such an extent that he became the supreme god representing the entire universe. His sanctuaries have been found from Asia to Israel, from Egypt to Greece, and from Italy, where he was known as "Faunus", into Russia. If Walker is correct his influence, if not his origin, was also felt in the Indian subcontinent.

It may be that the Christians created Satan out of the image of Pan because Pan also gave freedom, freedom of choice and sexual freedom. Many patriarchal religions condemn these freedoms even today. His love of dance and music was well known. It was said that you did not approach his altars or temples quietly but with song and dance.

Pan was also closely associated with water. Many of his temples have been found in various grottos with natural springs or along rivers. One such place is known as the Golden Spring. Located along the Hyllikos River near Argolis, the Golden Spring "gushes down onto a ledge in the hillside shaded by plane trees, about forty or fifty feet above the level of the river, into which it then steeply pours. There is a stone bridge," writes Harry Brewster, "in one single piece leading over the stream a few yards away from the spring, known as the Devil's Bridge. ...a few paces from the spring and forming part of the site are several small niches carved in the porous face of the overhanging rock, which must have contained figurines and offerings." [169]

The bridge was named after the Devil due to an imprint in the stone of a cloven hoof. Brewster noted, "I cannot help feeling that if a

[169] Brewster, Harry. *The River Gods of Greece: Myths and Mountain Waters in the Hellenic World.* London: I.B. Tauris Publishers 1997, 65

live cloven foot ever left this imprint, it was Pan's rather than the Devil's, for the place is saturated with an atmosphere of Pan far removed from the world of the Christian Devil." [170]

The belief in the divinity of Pan cannot be doubted. An early tradition of the Christian faith states that Pan died at the same exact moment that Jesus was crucified. While this may have heralded the end of Paganism as an ancient religion, it also implies that Pan and Jesus were on the same level and that the world mourned for both. When it was announced that the Great God Pan was dead "there arose...a great cry of grief not from one person but of many, mingled with exclamations of dismay." [171]

That Pan was the god of nature is obvious but he was also much more. Pan was known as the god of healing and would come to those in need through dreams, advising the ill and the tormented on how to be cured.

Over time, other horned gods came to be recognized, especially in Europe. To the Celts Cernunnos was champion of the wild while Herne the Hunter became much feared during the Middle Age. While Pan was a half-man, half-goat figure Cernunnos was usually depicted as a man with long hair and beard and with the horns of a stag. Herne is similarly described but Herne was said to have a darker purpose, riding at night with baying dogs in search of souls. Cernunnos was undoubtedly the Celtic Pan and Herne was Pan evolving into a devilish

---

[170] Ibid
[171] Plutarch. De defectu oraculorum, 419b-e

figure as a response to Church teachings during the Middle Ages. Many of the Gods of Nature, however, have been depicted in story and image as hunters of the souls of men. Gwynn ap Nudd is one. As Lord of the Dead and the Underworld, he is also lord of the wild. Such tales undoubtedly date back to a pre-agricultural age when hunting, shamanism and animal totems were important aspects of religious beliefs. As agriculture became more widespread these tales changed and while the gods of vegetation became more pronounced they did not completely replace the older gods. "As the shaman's proto-myth is that of the hunt and its magic quarry," writes Ward Rutherford, "the agriculturalist's tells of the young god, personification of both the sun and dormant seed, who dies, descends to the Underworld, to be found and brought back to life…" [172]

The image of Cernunnos on the famous 2nd century BCE Gundestrup Cauldron is almost identical to that of the Lord of Animals, Pashupati from Mohenjo Daro in India testifying to a common source.

The Green Man is another variation of the Great God Pan. Dione Fortune, the founder of the Western Esoteric Tradition wrote in her novel, *The Goat Foot God:*

"I suppose you know who the Green Man is? He's Pan…He's Jack-In-The-Green, the wood-spirit—the fairy man who runs after the

---

[172] Rutherford, Ward. *Celtic Lore: The history of the Druids and their timeless traditions.* London: Thorsons/Aquarian 1993, 47

maidens on midsummer eve—What's that but Pan?...Pan is the same everywhere. He's elemental force—". [173]

The worship of Pan, according to writer Charles G. Leland, continued at least into the 19th century in Italy among the peasant populations. "Whoever would beg a favour of him", wrote Leland, "must go in the evening, and kneel to him in a field by the light of the moon…". [174]

Adonis, Attis & Tammuz: Gods of Vegetation

Adonis, the beautiful young god of Greek mythology is rarely recognized today as a far older god whose origin perhaps rests with the Sumerians. Simply put his name means "lord" or "my lord". Adonis is one of the young sacrificed gods of vegetation. He died on or near the date of the Spring Equinox, close to the date that Christians have determined to be Easter. He was born of the Divine Father and the virgin Myrrha who had turned to a tree. Like Jesus, Adonis was born in Bethlehem. Frazer, citing Jerome, wrote, "he tells us that Bethlehem, the traditionary birthplace of the Lord, was shaded by a grove of that still older Syrian Lord, Adonis, and that where the infant Jesus had wept, the lover of Venus was bewailed….If Adonis was indeed…the spirit of the corn, a more suitable name for his dwelling-place could

---

[173] Fortune, Dione. *The Goat Foot God*. York Beach: Samuel Wiser, Inc. 1980, 165. A reprint of the 1936 edition.
[174] Leland, Charles G. *Etruscan Roman Remains*. Blaine: Phoenix Publishing Inc., n/d , 46. A reprint of the 1892 edition.

hardly be found than Bethlehem, 'the house of Bread'…". [175] After his death, Adonis was buried in a cave—much like Jesus and other savior gods. His birth and death are symbolic of the spring growth of vegetation and the decay of vegetation in the winter—but the promise of his death is the rebirth, the renewal of that very same vegetation. Adonis has been known by other names as well. We also know that Adonis was remembered well into the early 20th century. Frazer wrote in 1932 "we are able to show that the gardens of Adonis…are still planted, first, by a primitive race at their sowing season, and, second, by European peasants at midsummer. Amongst the Oraons and Mundas of Begnal, when the time comes for planting…a party of young people of both sexes go to the forest and cut a young Karma-tree…Bearing it in triumph they return, dancing, singing, and beating drums, and plant it in the middle of the village dancing-ground. A sacrifice is offered to the tree: the next morning the youth of both sexes, linked arm-in-arm, dance in a great circle round the Karma-tree, which is decked with strips of coloured cloth…bracelets and necklets of plaited straw." [176] The Greeks knew him as Adonis but his older form was Tammuz, as the Babylonians knew him. Tammuz was the consort of Ishtar (also known as Inanna in Summeria)—the Great Goddess, the Earth Mother. Ishtar was the embodiment of the fertile powers of nature.

---

[175] Frazer, Sir. J. G. *Adonis: A Study in the History of Oriental Religion*. London: Watts & Co. 1932, 217
[176] Ibid, 200

"Every year", wrote Frazer, "Tammuz was believed to die, passing away from the cheerful earth to the gloomy subterranean world." [177] Inanna/Ishtar journeyed to the world of the dead to bring Tammuz back, for in his absence "love ceased to operate: men and beast alike forgot to reproduce their kinds: all life was threatened with extinction."[178] The queen of the underworld allowed Inanna to sprinkle Tammuz with the Water of Life so that the two could return to the upper world to revive nature. He was able to spend half the year above the land of the dead in the sunlight and the world rejoiced. The other half he resided in the land of the dead and the world mourned and died as well in the cold, dark months. Among the Babylonians Tammuz was called "Healer", "Savior", "Heavenly" and "Good Shepherd", among the Sumerians he was known as "my Christ."[179] He was also known as the corn-spirit.

The popularity of Adonis/Tammuz was such that the entire Mediterranean world mourned his death on an annual basis. In fact, his wide spread popularity is inferred in the one reference of Tammuz in the Old Testament. In Ezekiel 8:14 Ezekiel states "then he brought me to the door of the gate of the Lord's house which was toward the north; and, behold, there sat women weeping for Tammuz." This passage indicates that even Hebrew women held Tammuz/Adonis as a

---

[177] Ibid, 6
[178] Frazer, Sir James. *The Golden Bough: A Study in Magic and Religion.* Hertforsdhire: Wordsworth Editions Ltd., 1993, 326
[179] Ibid., 971

divine being and his death was mourned at the gate of the temple of Jerusalem. Frazier indicates that the Jewish priesthood, at one time, continued the far older rites of the Canaanites and actually portrayed the living Adonis in ritual—thus the weeping women were participants of the cultural and religious traditions.[180] Women observed the death of Tammuz and his resurrection each year at harvest, identifying with Inanna and her loss they would lament with cries of "Tammuz, Tammuz, Tammuz the all-great is dead". They would then plant "gardens, pots of flowers and herbs that—like the god and the vegetation he represented—swiftly bloom, wither, and die."[181]

Mackenize believed that the myth of Tammuz "was fully developed at the dawn of history". [182] This is probably correct as other gods such as Attis, Dionysus and Osiris are simply other personifications of Tammuz and, while they are ancient deities, their stories come well after those of Tammuz.

Attis dies beneath a pine tree or, in other myths; he is crucified on such a tree. Bandages used in the attempt to stop his bleeding were hung from the branches. This has probably continued in the present day tradition of Christmas tree decorations as well as the hanging of "clooties" (strips of cloth) from trees near holy wells. Historian Franz Cumont wrote of the annual rituals surrounding Attis:

---

[180] Ibid, 12

[181] Hallam, Elizabeth. *Gods and Goddesses*. New York: Macmillan 1996, 77

[182] Mackenize, Donald A. *Crete & Pre-Hellenic Myths and Legends*. London: Senate 1995, 164 (A reprint of the 1917 publication published by The Gresham Publishing Company, London)

"The ceremonies proper began with the equinox. A pine was felled and transferred to the temple of the Palatine by a brotherhood that owed to this function its name of 'tree-bearers'. Wrapped like a corpse in woolen bands and garlands of violets, this pine represented Attis dead. This god was originally only the spirit of the plants, and the honors given to the 'March-tree' in front of the imperial palace perpetuated a very ancient agrarian rite of the Phrygian peasants." [183]

Wherever traditions existed of the young male sacrificial god, they are always linked to the Great Goddess. As Cumont noted concerning the annual rituals mourning the death of Attis, "then followed a mysterious vigil during which the mystic was supposed to be united as a new Attis with the great goddess."[184] These traditions existed at least in 3000 BCE Egypt, ancient Sumer, Bablyon, Canaan and Anatolia. As noted, the annual lamentations and mourning for Tammuz were practiced even outside the gates of the Temple of Jerusalem and in pre-Christian Rome where, Merlin Stone notes, the rituals performed there "possibly...influencing the symbolism and rituals of early Christianity." [185]

John Barleycorn & Jack-In-The-Green

Barley is perhaps the oldest grown cereal product on earth. Because of its lengthy history and usage, it also figured as an important

---

[183] Cumont, Franz. *Oriental Religions in Roman Paganism.* New York: Dover Publications 1956, 56 (A reprint of the 1911 edition published by C. Routledge & Sons, Ltd.)
[184] Ibid, 57
[185] Stone, Merlin. *When God Was A Woman.* New York: Barnes & Noble Books 1993, 20

religious symbol, depicted as an agricultural deity. Likewise, corn may be the oldest cultivated vegetation in the world and was responsible for the settlement of humans in the first villages, cities and kingdoms. The importance of both cannot be overestimated.

The Jack-in-the-Green figure reportedly dates back at least to medieval days. A village youth, on May Day, parades through town dressed in a costume that totally encases him in a wicker framework entwined in ribbons, flowers and ivy. Jack-in-the-Green is, according to Frazer, "the spirit of vegetation". [186] The figure of Jack is closely associated with the chimney sweep. First described in print in 1801 the Jack/sweep connection would seem to be rather vague. Matthews writes that the sweeps are associated with good luck and the otherworld as well as with ancient sacrificial burnings. [187] Like the Green Man, Jack-in-the-Green also has his detractors. Trubshaw states that he was purely 18th century entertainment, devised to pry the halfpence from the hands of the revelers. [188]

Trubshaw's argument is that the need for sweeps did not arise until the early 18th century so the Jack-in-the-Green figure most likely did not predate that age. Trubshaw bases his conclusion on a small work called *The Jack-in-the-Green: A May Day Custom* written by Roy Judge and published in 1979. However, there remains a large amount of historical

---

[186] Frazer, Sir James. *The Golden Bough: A Study in Magic and Religion.* Hertfordshire: Wordsworth Editions LTD. 1993, 129
[187] Matthews, John. *The Quest for the Green Man.* Wheaton: Quest Books 2001, 74
[188] Trubshaw, Bob. "Paganism in British Folk Customs" in *At the Edge*, No. 3, 1996

references with long established traditions around the world of similar Jack figures and festivals. It is unlikely that a regional bit of entertainment would have been so widely dispersed at that time in the world without some ancient causation. Early 20th century writers attribute Jack-in-the-Green to an ancient pagan survival. W.Y. Evans-Wentz wrote in 1911: "...in many parts of modern England, the Jack-in-the-Green, a man entirely hidden in a covering of green foliage who dances through the streets on May Day, may be another example of a very ancient tree (or else agriculture) cult of Celtic origin." [189]

John Barleycorn is often mentioned as another name for Jack-in-the-Green; however, there appear to be enough differences to discuss him separately. John Barleycorn is the personification of barley, a true vegetation god. Unlike the Green Man, there are many examples of female corn spirits such as the Corn Queen, Corn Mother, and the Corn-maiden. All of theses spirits die at the hands of man, only to be reborn once again. John Barleycorn is another sacrificed king who returns in the following year to bring abundance and fertility to the crops. An 18th century English folksong, written by Robert Burns (1759-1796) sums up the story of John Barleycorn:

"There was three kings into the east,

Three kings both great and high,

And they hae sworn a solemn oath

---

[189] Evans-Wentz, W.Y. *The Fairy-Faith in Celtic Countries*. Mineola: Dover Publications, Inc. 2002, 435. A reprint of the 1911 edition published by Henry Frowde, London.

John Barleycorn should die.

"They took a plough and plough'd him down,

Put clods upon his head,

And they hae sworn a solemn oath

John Barleycorn was dead.

"But the cheerful Spring came kindly on,

And show'rs began to fall;

John Barleycorn got up again,

And sore surpris'd them all."

Festivals, which are still held year after year, indicate that the survival of these ancient figures is deeply rooted in the collective minds and souls of all of us. It was common in the United States until the middle of the 20th century to find Maypole festivals held, at least in schools, on Arbor Day. This event has recently been revived in some areas of the United States, including the small town of Toledo, Oregon. Other festivals include The Burry Man festival. This custom, which used to occur annually on August 3rd, is now held the second Friday in August in South Queensferry, Scotland. An individual, who must have been born in the town, is elected annually by the Ferry Fair Committee to be the Burry Man.

The chosen man is covered in a layer of flannel, which is then covered in burrs from the burdock. Today the Burry Man walks 7 miles from one boundary of Queensferry to the other and it is a time of strange celebration. People dress is disguises, perambulate around and collect money. While he resembles the Green Man he is, like

Green Jack (Jack-in-the-Green) acting as a scapegoat. During his walk, he is absorbing the sins of the population that stick to him like the burrs. "Another theory", according to Brian Day, "connects him with an old ceremony to ensure good herring catches, as a similar figure existed in the north-eastern Scottish ports of Buckie and Fraserburgh. As the burrs stick to the netting, so may fish, and he may have been called upon to remove the ill luck following poor catches." [190] Similar rituals have also been held in France and Germany.

All of these mythic figures may represent the collective memory of a time when individuals were selected as sacrificial kings to be, after being treated as royalty for a year, decapitated to ensure the survival and prosperity of the group. One festival still held annually is that of the Garland King who was a central figure in the springtime celebrations throughout Britain and Northern and Central Europe. Held in Castleton, the festival appears to be a mixture of older May Day celebrations, which had been banned by the Puritans during the Reformation, and to mark the return of Charles II after his defeat at the Battle of Worcester in 1651. The date of the original Garland festival is unknown but the first printed reference to it was in 1749.

Held on May 29 as "Oak-apple Day", the event has only survived into modern days in Cornwall. Many believe that the Garland festival contains ancient survivals of tree worship and of the sacrificial king. [191]

---

[190] Day, Brian. *Chronicle of Celtic Folk Customs*. London: Hamlyn 2000, 136
[191] Ibid

The Garland King, dressed head to foot in garlands of flowers and greenery, is symbolically decapitated at the end of a long day of parades, dancing, and visits to the pubs. "The remainder of the garland", writes Fran and Geoff Doel, "is hoisted up the church tower and displayed for a week on one of the pinnacles of the tower, all the other pinnacles being decorated with sycamore." [192] The day ends with young girls dancing around the maypole.

Hun Hunahpu and the Gods of Mesoamerica

Thus far, we have only examined the vegetation gods of Europe but there are far more. Native Americans in both North and South America worshipped maize gods and many of the images carved of deities in Mesoamerica depict them with maize, vines and other plant life sprouting from their heads in mimicry of the Green Man in the northern latitudes. "Representations of the maize plant", wrote archaeologist Robert Rands, "are commonly depicted as growing from the head of the Maize God, while with equal certainty water lilies emerge from the heads of other beings." [193] Mayan carvings actually depict three types of Maize God. One from the Early Classic Period is of a young man with maize leaves sprouting from the top of his head, the "Tonsured Maize God" is associated with one of the Hero Twins

---

[192] Doel, Fran & Geoff. *The Green Man in Britain*. Gloucestershire: Tempus Publishing Ltd. 2001, 103

[193] Rands, Robert L. "Some Manifestations of Water in Mesoamerican Art" in *Anthropological Papers Numbers 43-48, Smithsonian Institution Bureau of American Ethnology Bulletin 157*. Washington: US Government Printing Office 1955, 331-332

and the other, referred to as the "Foliated Mazie God has a solitary ear of maize springing from his head. Hun Hunahpu is one of these important vegetation gods.

According to the *Popol Vuh*, the most important sacred book still surviving of the Quiché Maya, Hun Hunahpu was the father of the Hero Twins, Xbalanque and Hunahpu and the Monkey Scribe twins Hun Batz and Hun Chuen. Hun Hunahpu and his brother, Vucab Hunahpu are defeated in a battle with the gods of death and are sacrificed in the underworld. In Mayan art the head of Hun Hunahpu is depicted resting in a tree that suddenly and magically is transformed into a gourd. The spittle from the head impregnates the maiden Xquic and she gives birth to the Hero Twins who eventually defeat the gods of death and resurrect Hun Hunahpu and his brother. In some Mayan carvings, Hun Hunahpu's head is shown in a cacao tree and is depicted as turning into a cacao pod. Like the other Green Gods, Hun Hunahpu is a vegetation god. Miller and Taube note, "in many vessel scenes he emerges from the earth, much like planted corn sprouting out of the soil."[194] There are several things in this bit of lore that are also common among lore of the Green Man and myths of other cultures. Hun Hunahpu is decapitated, he is resurrected from the underworld, and he is intimately associated with trees and vegetation. He is a symbol of the renewal of life after death.

---

[194] Miller, Mary and Karl Taube. *An Illustrated Dictionary of the Gods and Symbols of Ancient Mexico and the Maya.* New York: Thames and Hudson 1993, 98

The Corn or Maize god is widespread throughout Native American and Mesoamerican culture. The importance of maize can hardly be understated. "Man and maize and world", wrote Hartley Alexander, "are ultimately one inter-substantiate being."[195] To American Indians the ear of corn and all of its kernels represented all the people of the earth and all of the things in the universe. Ears of corn were also sacred to the Egyptians, Greeks, and Romans and to the Sumero-Semitic peoples who attributed corn to Tammuz. Foremost corn represents fertility and abundance.

It was not Tammuz however whom American Indians worshiped as the deity of corn. It was Mother Corn. Mother Corn was the source of wisdom and intelligence, the provider of sustenance, life-giver and guardian as well as the guide of humankind. Like the other Lords of the Wild, Mother Corn not only offered protection to man but to all animals no less so. However, she also provides game for the hunt. Among the Arikara, it was said, "Father Heaven placed Mother Corn in authority over all things on this Earth. She moves between men and the Spirit Above from whom all things come."[196]

The Pueblo Indians, the Hopi and Navajo are famous for their Corn Dances but the Delaware also honor the Maize Mother with festival. According to lore "some childish abuse of the maize once provoked her [Maize Mother's] wrath, and she sent down a terrible

---

[195] Alexander, Hartley Burr. *The World's Rim: Great Mysteries of the North American Indians.* Mineola: Dover Publications Inc., 1999, 78 (A reprint of the 1953 edition published by the University of Nebraska Press)
[196] Ibid., 31

sickness."[197] To appease the Maize Mother a nocturnal doll dance is performed "in which the maize mother herself, in the form of a corn doll,[198] is fed with flesh and hominy and honoured in twelve dances, one for each month."[199] As part of the ceremony large figures in the form of the Maize Mother and of a bear are baked from maize flower. These are tossed crosswise between two rows of participants who then take pieces of the figures home with them.

It is interesting to note that corn has a long association with marriage in other parts of the world such as Great Britain. Thompson says, "the wedding or bride's cake is a survival of the symbolic corn-ears originally worn by the bride." [200] Thompson also says that in "later times" the cakes were scattered over the heads of the newly married couple after their return from church. It can be assumed that the corn cakes continued to preserve the sacredness of the act of marriage and associated fertility.

The Peruvian Indians also represented the Corn Mother in doll form. The doll, made from corn ears and leaves, was dressed in full

---

[197] Krickeberg, Walter & et al. *Pre-Columbian American Religions.* New York: Holt, Rinehart and Winston History of Religion Series 1969, 167

[198] Similar corn dolls used by the Delaware were also commonly made in Europe in the 19th century. Frazer wrote that in Perthshire "the last handful of corn is cut by the youngest girl...and is made into the rude form of a female doll, clad in paper dress, and checked with ribbons. It is called the Maiden, and is kept in the farmhouse, generally above the chimney,...sometimes till the Maiden of the next year is brought in." (The Golden Bough: The Roots of Religion and Folklore. New York: Avenel Books 1981, 345)

[199] Krickeberg, op cit..

[200] Thompson, C.J.S. *The Hand of Destiny: Everyday Folklore and Superstitions.* London: Senate 1995, 61 (A reprint of the 1932 edition published by Rider & Company, London)

female garb. The Peruvians believed that the doll "had the power of producing and giving birth to much maize."[201]

The Peruvian dolls were kept for a year but they were asked periodically how they felt and if the doll indicated that it was becoming weak it would be burned and another made to take its place. In this way, the Maize Mother also became a sacrificial god, as were the male gods of vegetation in other parts of the world.

In Lakota belief, an ear of corn is much more. In the Hunka ceremony, it is used for "giving a particular relationship to two persons"—much as corn was used in wedding ceremonies in Britain in the 19th century. However, in this ceremony the relationship established is like father and son or brother and sister. The shaman secretly selects the ear of corn and he "subdues its…potency by his mystic powers and…compels it to do his will."[202] This ear of corn symbolizes the Great God—the Earth.

Corn Woman, also in Lakota tradition, acts as a guardian and facilitator of the spirit world. Corn Woman, called *Irriaku*, "maintains the connection between the non-human supernaturals and the tribe." [203] Irriaku is also "the heart of the people" and she appears in every tribal ceremony as a perfect ear of corn. According to Paula Gunn Allen who is not only a teacher of Native American studies but a Sioux

---

[201] Frazer, op cit. 351
[202] Walker, James R. *Lakota Belief and Ritual.* Lincoln: University of Nebraska Press 1991, 217
[203] Allen, Paula Gunn. *The Sacred Hoop: Recovering the Feminine in American Indian Traditions.* Boston: Beacon Press 1986, 17

Indian herself, "without the presence of her power, no ceremony can produce the power it is designed to create or release." [204]

Like other gods of the forest and vegetation, Corn Woman is the most important link between the spirit world and the world of humankind.

In the folklore of the Popoluca Indians of Veracruz, Mexico, it is a small boy who is recognized as the "Man of Crops". In the myth, the boy asks his father to kill him, saying that he did not want to live anymore but that he would be born again in the form of crops. "I am the one who is going to give food to all mankind, I am he who sprouts at the knees." [205] The Man of Crops is also prominent in Aztec, Tepecano and Tarascan mythology where, after he is buried, corn and tobacco grows from his grave. In contemporary Quiché mythology, crops spill from the body of Jesus immediately following his crucifixion. In these examples, it can be seen that the savior god is universally linked to vegetation with the sprouting of plants from the body of the fallen god.

Asherah

Until now, we have primarily focused on the male gods of vegetation. For one reason this is because only the male gods are universally known as sacrificial gods that must die for the sins of the world and are then reborn—mimicking the annual death and rebirth of

---

[204] Ibid.
[205] Bierhorst, John. *The Mythology of Mexico and Central America*. New York: William Morrow and Company Inc. 1990, 68

nature. While we have and will continue to acknowledge the ties of trees and vegetation with goddesses, there is truly only one that needs to have some in-depth discussion. That one is Asherah. To the ancient Canaanites, it was Asherah who provided the continuation of all life.

Known by the names Astarte, Aphrodite, Isis, Hathor and Ishtar in other parts of the world, Asherah, meaning "grove", was the Semitic name for the Great Goddess. She was also referred to as the Tree of Life and the Queen of Heaven. Asherah was foremost a Babylonian-Canaanite Goddess who, over time, was also worshipped by the Hebrews as their chief deity. It was probably Solomon who introduced her to the Hebrews around 1000 BCE and installed her in the Temple of Jerusalem. [206] A tree or carved wooden pillar was erected in every temple to represent her. "It was a conventionalized or stylized tree", wrote Monica Sjöö, "perceived as she, and planted therefore at all altars and holy places. This *asherah* represented the Goddess as Urikittu, the green one, the Neolithic mother-daughter of all vegetation." [207] Asherah was worshipped from the Neolithic and Bronze Ages through the Early Iron Age as evidenced by plaques, amulets and the hundreds of figurines recovered in most every excavation undertaken in Palestine. [208]

---

[206] Patai, Raphael. *The Hebrew Goddess*. New York: Avon Books 1978, 23

[207] Sjöö, Monica & Barbara Mor. *The Great Cosmic Mother: Rediscovering the Religion of the Earth*. New York: Harper Collins 1991, 269

[208] James, E. O. *The Cult of the Mother-Goddess*. New York: Barnes & Noble Books 1994, 69

The wooden posts, referred to as *asherah*, not only stood by the altars but also by the stone megaliths that were erected in the sanctuaries where the traditional religious rites were performed. These asherah not only represented the Goddess, but her spirit was believed to inhabit them as well. Asherah was so important to the Hebrews that her asherah pillars were prominently placed in the Temple of Jerusalem. Some researchers, such as Merlin Stone, believe that the asherah "were actually fig trees, the sycamore fig, the tree that was in Egypt considered to be the 'Body of the Goddess on Earth'". [209]

The Hebrews predominately worshipped Asherah from the earliest date of their occupation of Canaan until the destruction of Jerusalem almost 600 years later. The male god, Yahweh was only superficially considered at all, and at that as a consort of Asherah. It was only by force that the monotheistic patriarchal priesthood replaced Asherah. [210] The monotheists slaughtered entire towns and the Bible provides evidence of the forces involved. In Deuteronomy 12:2 Yahweh commands the priests thusly: "You shall surely destroy all the places where the nations who you shall dispossess served their gods, upon the high mountains and upon the hills and under every green tree you shall tear down their pillars and burn their asherim with fire." According to James, the popular following of Asherah was so great, even after the butchery, that the standing of the patriarchal Yahweh was compromised: "such was the strength of the Canaanite cult (of

---

[209] Stone, op cit 175
[210] Patai, op cit 16

Asherah) that Yahweh from being a desert god was transformed virtually into a vegetation deity." [211]

Tree Spirits and Tree Dwellers

Trees are wondrous creatures. Certain trees have been known throughout time as the Tree of Life and the Tree of Knowledge. Trees have created a sense of awe in the minds of humankind since abstract thought was possible. To many, trees were the source of life and fertility. Trees not only were rooted in the Mother Earth but also reached into the heavens. Trees became symbols of stability and immortality. Because of this sense of awe, the tree has been worshipped and condemned, nurtured and felled. These senses of awe and fear have also created a host of other creatures that are closely associated with the tree and the forests. Most cultures have myths of tree gods and tales of strange fairy-like creatures that live deep in dark forests or in the very trees themselves. Such stories reflect an ancient animistic belief system that gives every object in nature its own spirit and power. As will be discussed later, these vegetation spirits and gods are the foundations for classic and contemporary religious thought.

Tree and Forest Spirits

The very *feel* of the forest imparts a sense of wonder and hidden power, of spirits and unseen creatures, and of a time stretching back into the dim past where anything and everything was possible. "The edge of the forest" writes Carol and Dinah Mack, "is always the

---

[211] James, op cit 79

boundary between the wild and domesticated, the animal and the human community. It holds its genius loci, which may appear as demonic guardian species of wilderness and wild creatures and attack trespassing hunters, mischievous fairies...and the many huge man-eating species...". [212] This statement may be applied to any forest in the world, for they all seem to be populated with these local spirits and fairies who are not often kind to human intrusion. The Cherokee, according to anthropologist James Mooney, believed that "trees and plants also were alive and could talk in the old days, and had their place in council". [213] The intelligence of trees and plants, as well as other inanimate objects, were taken for granted by the Cherokee and the other indigenous people around the world.

The Lakota believed in a race of "ugly" small men and women that they referred to as "tree dwellers". Similar to tales of other Fairy folk around the world, the tree dwellers, called *Can Otidan*, reportedly stayed in the woods and forests and "would lure hunters away and lose them or they would frighten them so that they would lose their senses." [214] The *Can Otidan* apparently were more than simple Fairy spirits as they were classed in a group referred to as "bad gods".

---

[212] Mack, Carol K. and Dinah Mack. *A Field Guide to Demons, Fairies, Fallen Angels, and Other Subversive Spirits.* New York: Owl Books 1998, 91

[213] Mooney, James. *Myths of the Cherokee.* New York: Dover Publications Inc. 1995 (A reprint of the *Nineteenth Annual Report of the Bureau of American Ethnology 1897-98* published in1900 by the Smithsonian Institution), 231

[214] Walker, James R. *Lakota Belief and Ritual.* Lincoln: University of Nebraska Press 1991, 107

Little people[215] referred to as "travel-two" were among the forest spirits in the Nehalem Tillamook (Oregon) world. Called "travel-two" because they always traveled in pairs, these fairy-like creatures were hunters and would often give a human they encountered on their travels the skills to become a good hunter—if they happened to speak to him. [216]

The Coos Indians along Oregon's southern coast believed that the forests were filled with ghosts and spirits. There were five types of spirits identified as residing in the forest:

1. Ghosts or spirits that "reentered a corpse and escaped into the forest to do evil things to humans, especially poor people",

2. A "mirror image" of oneself, a doppelganger, indicating that, if you see one of these, your life is shortened,

3. Giant people who live on the fish in the streams that are neither good nor bad "and do not scare people",

4. A visible spirit or ghost, and

5. The "noisy ones" that are the little people usually covered in long hair that leave tracks along creek banks. These creatures are usually seen only at night and are known to throw rocks at people's homes. [217]

---

[215] Other "little folk" in Tillamook lore are the ditʹkátu who lived in lakes. He is described as "like a little brownie, about one and a half feet high."

[216] Jacobs, Elizabeth D. *The Nehalem Tillamook: An Ethnography*. Corvallis: Oregon State University Press 2003, 182

[217] Beckham, Stephen Dow. "Coos, Lower Umpqua, and Siuslaw: Traditional Religious Practices" in *Native American Religious Practices and Uses, Siuslaw National Forest*. Eugene: Heritage Research Associates Report No. 7(3), September 20, 1982, 41

Other Oregonian tribes such as the Alsea and Yaquina believed in longhaired female wood sprites called *osun* who could give certain special powers to humans that would enable them to become shamans.[218]

The Russians as well had their own form of *Can Otidan*. Called the *Leshy*[219], these mysterious creatures inhabit the forests (mostly forests of birch trees) and they disappear and reappear with the falling leaves and the sprouting vegetation. Philpot described them as having "human form, with horns, ears, and feet of a goat, his fingers are long claws, and he is covered with rough hair, often of a green colour." [220] Some have described them as having green, bark-like skin and green hair. They could also change their stature at will, remaining as small as grass stalks or as tall as the tallest tree. Each spring the *Leshy* would awaken from its hibernation and seek out travelers to cause them to become lost in the new and rich growth of vegetation. "He springs from tree to tree, and rocks himself in the branches, screeching and laughing, neighing, lowing, and barking."[221] The trees and animals of the forest, however, are under his protection. Philpot wrote, "the migrations of squirrels, field-mice, and such small deer are carried out under his guidance."[222] The animals protected the Leshy as well as he

---

[218] Ibid., 27
[219] Also spelled as *Leshii*, or *Ljeschi*..
[220] Philpot, Mrs. J. H. *The Sacred Tree in Religion and Myth*. Mineola: Dover Publications Inc. 2004, 69 (A reprint of the 1897 edition published by Macmillan and Co. Ltd, New York & London)
[221] Ibid.
[222] Ibid.

was prone to drinking and vulnerable to attacks from other woodland spirits. "Uprooted trees, broken branches and other storm damage were a clear indication that *leshie* had been fighting among themselves", wrote Michael Kerrigan. [223] The only way to protect yourself from the Leshy while traveling through the forest was to wear your clothing inside out, shoes on the wrong feet, continuously making the sign of the cross or making peace offerings of tobacco and food.

The person who was most in danger from the wrath of the Leshy was the woodcutter. Even though this tree spirit was greatly feared, if one dared he could also be summoned. According to Porteous, "very young Birches are cut down and placed in a circle with the points towards the center. They then enter the circle and invoke the spirit, which at once appears. Then they step on the stump of one of the cut trees with their face turned towards the east, and bend their heads so that they look between their legs. While in this position they say: 'Uncle Lieschi, ascend thou, not as a grey wolf, not as an ardent fire, but as resembling myself'. Then the leaves tremble, and the Lieschi arises under a human form, and agrees to give service for which he has been invoked, provided they promise him their soul." [224] As in many cultures eventually dominated by the Christian church the spirits and deities of the Slavs were changed. As Porteous noted above, the

---

[223] Charles Phillips & Michael. *Forests of the Vampire: Slavic Myth.* New York: Barnes & Noble Books 1999, 72

[224] Porteous, Alexander. *The Lore of the Forest: Myths and Legends.* London: Senate 1996, 105 (A reprint of *Forest Folklore* published in 1928 by George Allen & Unwin Ltd., London)

Lieschie bargained for the soul of the person in exchange for supernatural aid and acted as an acolyte of Satan.

Another Russian vegetation entity is the "polevoi". Michael Kerrigan wrote that the polevoi's body "matched the colour of the local soil, and grass grew in tussocks from his head instead of hair." [225] The polevoi could be friendly to humans but could signify disaster as well should one spot him in the forest.

Tree elves are said to inhabit the elm, oak, willow, yew, fir, holly, pine, ash, cherry, laurel, nut, apple, birch and cypress trees. Because each of the tree elves is created from the specific tree, it takes on the characteristics of that tree. While all of these species of trees have a resident elf, "the elder", writes Nancy Arrowsmith, "has without doubt the highest elf population." [226] The lives of the "elder elves" are tied directly to their tree and so they are very protective of it. According to German folklore one should always ask permission (and be sure to leave an offering!) before cutting or otherwise harming an elder. The consequences of not doing so are usually serious and can result in blindness or ill health to the woodsman's children or cattle. The appearance of tree elves varies according to the tree from which they originated. The oak elf will appear as a gnarled old man and the birch elf appears as a thin white female.

---

[225] Kerrigan, Michael. "The Harvester of Souls" in *Forests of the Vampire: Slavic Myth*. New York: Barnes & Noble 2003, 74

[226] Arrowsmith, Nancy and George Moorse. *A Field Guide to the Little People*. London: Macmillan Company 1977, 180

In England, an Apple Tree Man was said to reside in the oldest apple tree in each orchard. According to Franklin, "He can grant a good harvest for the whole orchard, and other benefits besides. The last of the crop should be left on the ground for him..." [227]

To the Saxons elves were to be feared. They were "hostile creatures [that] brought disease...as well as nightmare." [228]

The belief that trees are somehow supernatural beings is universal. Ozark lore says that agents of the Devil propagated the ironwood tree and that the sassafras tree does not grow from seeds, but rather "somehow sprout from grub worms." [229] The belief in "Devil Trees" was common in Africa and the Malay Archipelago. However, these trees are receptacles of evil and not sources of evil. Like the holy wells in England and elsewhere where people tie strips of cloth and ribbon, known as "clooties", to nearby trees, these Devil Trees are also sought out for this purpose. In both cases, the purpose is the same, to tie a piece of cloth that belongs to an ill person to the tree so that the disease is transferred from the human to the tree.

In Celtic lands, the gods were worshipped in sacred groves, which negated the need to have temple structures—although a few did exist. The Romans and then the Christians destroyed these groves in their attempts to destroy the fabric of Celtic pagan traditions. However,

---

[227] Franklin, Anna. *The Illustrated Encyclopaedia of Fairies*. London: Paper Tiger/Chrysalis Books 2004, 15

[228] Owen, Gale R. *Rites and Religions of the Anglo-Saxons*. Dorset Press 1985, 65

[229] Randolph, Vance. *Ozark Magic and Folklore*. New York: Dover Publications 1964, 261 (A reprint of *Ozark Superstitions* published by Columbia University Press 1947)

there is significant evidence that these groves, or rather their descendants, did survive into later ages in the form of "gospel oaks" in Britain and innumerable place names across Europe. Hutton writes that these groves, after Christianization, "kept their place in the sentiments of the tribes even while apparently losing all direct religious connotations." [230]

Because tree worship and sacred groves were so ingrained in the human mind, the Church fought long and hard to eliminate all aspects of them, passing law after law and levying heavy fines of those who continued to honor the tree. "S. Martin of Tours", wrote J.A. MacCulloch, "was allowed to destroy a temple, but the people would not permit him to attack a much venerated pine-tree which stood beside it—an excellent example of the way in which the more official paganism fell before Christianity, while the older religion of the soil from which it sprang, could not be entirely eradicated." [231]

The struggle to defeat and subjugate pagans who worshipped trees, or viewed them as sacred, or who believed that the gods live in certain trees, was not the only battle waged by the early Christians. H.R. Ellis Davidson reminds us, "a number of Christian missionaries...counted the felling of a tree sacred to a heathen god among their achievements

---

[230] Hutton, Ronald. *The Pagan Religions of the Ancient British Isles: Their Nature and Legacy.* Oxford: Blackwell Publishers Ltd.1991, 293

[231] MacCulloch, J.A. *The Religion of the Ancient Celts.* Mineola: Dover Publications, Inc. 2003, 204 (A reprint of the 1911 publication from T. & T. Clark, Edinburgh). Another version of this story is told by W.Y. Evans-Wentz in his book *The Fairy-Faith in Celtic Countries*, page 435: "The people agreed to let it be cut down on the condition that the saint should receive its great trunk on his head as it fell: and the tree was not cut down".

in the cause of Christ." [232] The early Jews also waged this battle. In Deuteronomy 12:2-3 God instructs the Hebrew leaders to "utterly destroy all the places, wherein the nations which ye shall possess served their gods, upon the high mountains, and upon the hills, and under every green tree.

"And ye shall overthrow their altars, and break their pillars, and burn their groves with fire…"

Because of this, the Hebrews were forbidden from planting any tree near a sacred altar.

In many cultures (among them the Nordic countries, Greeks, Romans, Iraqi and Iranians, Indian and Native Americans as well as some African tribes) it was said that humans were created from trees. Porteous noted, "among the South American tribes of Guiana a great creator is acknowledged. They say that all created things came from a branch of a Silk-cotton tree which had been cut down by the Creator, but that the white man had sprung from the chips of a particularly useless tree." [233]

In Norse mythology three Creator Gods walked on a seashore, where, according to Davidson, "they found two trees, driftwood washed ashore, breathed vitality and spirit into them, and gave them movement, so that the first man and woman came to life." [234]

---

[232] Davidson, H.R. Ellis. *Gods and Myths of the Viking Age.* New York: Bell Publishing Company 1981, 87

[233] Porteous, op cit., 160

[234] Davidson, H.R. Ellis. *Myths and Symbols in Pagan Europe: Early Scandinavian and Celtic Religions.* Syracuse: Syracuse University Press 1988, 173

The belief that humans came from trees is also widespread in Africa. John S. Mbiti wrote, "The Herero tell that God caused the first human beings, a man and his wife, to come from the mythical 'tree of life' which is said to be situated in the underworld." [235] Similar stories were common throughout Africa from Angola to Zambezi, the Congo and Sudan.

The stories that predominate, however, are those of the nature spirits, gods and goddesses that inhabit the tree. Frequent discussions were held in the days of early Buddhism as to whether trees had souls. It was decided then that trees do not have souls but that they may be inhabited by wood spirits that, at times, may speak through the trees. Other people however, such as the Tahitians and Greeks, did believe that each tree had a soul and an intellect of its own.

For some reason most tree-spirits are ambivalent at best and demonic at worst. Stories abound of tree-spirits that take savage revenge on those that dare to cut trees down. Indian legend says the Banyan tree is inhabited by spirits that will "wring the necks of all persons who approached their tree during the night." [236] The guardian spirit of the Brazilian rainforest is Corupira who is not evil but will disorient those who are intent on harming the trees and the forest animals—much like Pan. However, other tree and forest-spirits do exhibit traits of kindness towards humans. Some forest spirits were

---

[235] Mbiti, John S. *African Religions and Philosophy.* Garden City: Anchor Books 1970, 121
[236] Porteous, op cit 123.

said to protect hunters and fishers, and in fact leading game to them. It was to these spirit-gods that the forests were dedicated and sacrifices made. In other cultures, tree spirits provided the rains and sun that made crops grow.

The Mesquakie, known as the Fox Indians of Iowa, believed that the spirits of their ancestors lived within the trees. It was said, "the murmur of the trees when the wind passes through is but the voices of our grandparents." [237] The Fox felt that all wood was sacred and that objects made from wood "were thought to contain the very essence of a tree's spiritual substance."[238]

Nature spirits, normally described as miniature people but not necessarily the same as Fairy, are common throughout most third-world societies. This is not a judgment of those cultures only an observation that the more "developed" and "western" societies have lost this connection with nature. The Gururumba, a New Guinea people, believe in certain nature spirits, some who live in the forests and others who live in the reeds along the riverbanks. Other than the location of territory, there is little difference between the two forms of nature spirit. The Gururumba say that these spirits are seldom seen because even though they reside in our world, in our reality, they appear as mist or smoke. They are also always male. While generally ambivalent to the humans who live in the area the spirits will attack anyone who stumbles into their territory. Ethnologist Philip L.

---

[237] Anon. *The Spirit World*. Alexandria: Time-Life Books 1992, 90.
[238] Ibid.

Newman, who researched the Gururumba, writes "each spirit has its own dwelling place—a certain clump of reeds, a particular configuration of boulders along the river, or the exposed roots of some tree. Anyone wandering into one of these sanctuaries is attacked by the spirit which may cause him illness or even death." [239]

The Gururumba have created a cooperative arrangement with many of the nature spirits by providing a small dome-shaped house (about two feet in diameter) in an enclosure in the family garden. The Gururumba provide housing, food and information to the nature spirit in exchange for the spirit's protection of the garden and care for the Gururumba's pig herds.

Tree spirits are also commonly believed in throughout Africa. The Ashanti reportedly believe that certain nature spirits are present that animate trees, stones and other "inanimate" objects as well as animals, rivers and charms. The powers of these spirits are great and respected. John Mbiti reports in his book *African Religions and Philosophy* of an incident that took place in Ghana in the 1960's. During the construction of a new harbor at Tema, equipment was repeatedly stolen and a company investigator, and Englishman, was sent to look into it. After his investigation was over one of the European supervisors mentioned to him that a lone tree was causing him a great deal of trouble. All the other trees in the area had been cleared but this

---

[239] Newman, Philip L. *Knowing the Gururumba*. New York: Holt, Rinehart and Winston Case Studies in Cultural Anthropology 1965, 63.

one, which was relatively small, remained as all the heavy equipment stalled when approaching the tree. One of the African foremen said that the tree was magic and could not be removed unless the tree spirit could be persuaded to move on to another tree. A shaman was called in who sacrificed three sheep and poured three bottled of gin onto the roots of the tree as an offering. Evidently, the ritual worked as the machinery could be started. However, a few of the workers simply walked to the tree and were able to pull it up out of the earth. [240]

The Gods of Vegetation, discussed in another chapter, were all originally tree spirits who gave the gift of agriculture to humankind as well as learning, arts, and the other things that create civilization. They were also closely connected with death and the underworld.

The sycamore fig tree located in many desert areas of Egypt is said to be inhabited by goddesses. "These goddesses or spirits", Porteous noted, "sometimes manifest themselves, and…the head, or even the whole body, would emerge from the trunk of the tree, after a time re-entering it, being reabsorbed, or, as the Egyptian expression has it, the trunk *ate* it again." [241] The goddesses said to reside in the sycamore are Hathor (given the epithet "Lady of the Sycamore"), Nut, Selkit, and Isis. While certain male gods were also associated with trees, such as Osiris with the willow, Horus with the acacia and Wepwawet with the tamarisk), only these few goddesses were so closely associated with sacred trees. Like the carvings of females rising from vegetation found

---

[240] Mbiti op cit 255.
[241] Porteous, op cit 164.

in contemporary architecture, these goddesses were most often shown as a "composite of the upper body of the goddess rising from the trunk at the center of a tree." [242] In the Egyptian world, the maternal deities were the tree goddesses, offering food to the deceased or, in the case of a mural in the tomb of Tuthmosis III, nursed by Isis in the form of a sycamore tree.

Dryads, or tree goddesses in India, are often depicted giving the trunk of a tree a little kick. The reason for this, according to Heinrich Zimmer, is found in a formula derived "from a ritual of fecundation. According to an ageless belief, nature requires to be stimulated by man; the procreative forces have to be aroused, by magic means, from semi-dormancy." [243] This ritual formula continues to be used in contemporary Indian culture. Zimmer adds, "There is in India a certain tree (*aśoka*) which is supposed not to put forth blossoms unless touched and kicked by a girl or young woman. Girls and young women," Zimmer wrote, "are regarded as human embodiments of the maternal energy of nature. They are diminutive doubles of the Great Mother of all life, vessels of fertility, life in full sap, potential sources of new offspring. By touching and kicking the tree they transfer into it their potency, and enable it to bring forth blossom and fruit."[244]

---

[242] Wilkinson, Richard H. *The Complete Gods and Goddesses of Ancient Egypt.* London: Thames & Hudson Ltd. 2003, 169.
[243] Zimmer, Heinrich. *Myths and Symbols in Indian Art and Civilization.* Edited by Joseph Campbell. Princeton: Princeton University Press 1946, 69.
[244] Ibid.

The Persians as well, according to J.H. Philpot, "venerated trees as the dwelling-place of the deity, as the haunts of good and evil spirits, and as the habitations in which the souls of heroes and the virtuous dead continued their existence." [245]

In ancient Crete, the Great Mother goddess was also known as the Lady of Trees and Doves—representing birth and fertility. In her early form the Great Mother of Crete, the Earth Mother, was rather vague—she was an ancient Neolithic goddess. In time, she became Demeter, goddess of animals, crops and forests. [246]

The gods and goddesses also lived within the trees of old Hawaii. The goddess of the ohia-lehua forest is one of these. The flower of the ohia tree is considered sacred and to pick it is forbidden unless proper invocations are said. One of the sacred ohia trees located in a cave of the god Ku-ka-ohia-laka is regarded as the body of this forefather-god. [247] The Hawaiian wind god, Makani-keoe, is another tree deity. Also known as a "love god", he is able to transform himself into a tree at will. An amulet made from such a tree is a powerful love charm but causes visions and voices to be heard by the one who obtains it.

Sacred groves in Germany were the homes of the gods as well. At Romove, the chief sacred grove, a holy oak figured in religious

[245] Philpot, Mrs. J.H. *The Sacred Tree in Religion and Myth.* Mineola: Dover Publications, Inc. 2004, 13 (A reprint of the 1897 edition published by Macmillan and Co. Ltd, London and New York)
[246] Mackenzie, Donald A. *Crete & Pre-Hellenic Myths and Legends.* London: Senate 1995, 175 (A reprint of the 1917 publication by the Gresham Publishing Company, London)
[247] Beckwith, Martha. *Hawaiian Mythology.* Honolulu: University of Hawaii Press1970, 16-17 (A reprint of the 1940 edition published by Yale University Press)

ceremonies and images of the gods were placed in its trunk. The Prussians who remained Pagan long after the rest of Germany had converted to Christianity used these groves into the 16th century. Davidson notes "writers who visited them described sacred woods in which they made sacrifices and sacred springs which Christians were not allowed to approach." [248] The god worshipped in the Prussian groves was Perkuno—the thunder god. It is believed that the word "Perkuno" is related to the Latin "quercus" meaning oak. Sacred groves were still utilized in Estonia into the 18th century as well. Every Dying God, such as Osiris, Adonis, Attis, Dionysus and Jesus, died on a tree. Mediaeval Christian carvings of the Tree of the Living and the Dead (fruit of good and evil on opposite sides) depict Jesus as the trunk of the tree. [249]

Gautama Buddha is said to have been a tree-spirit "no less than forty-three times" in past incarnations. [250]

The Gururumba have created a cooperative arrangement with many of the nature spirits by providing a small dome-shaped house (about two feet in diameter) in an enclosure in the family garden. The Gururumba provide housing, food and information to the nature spirit in exchange for the spirit's protection of the garden and care for the Gururumba's herds of pigs.

---

[248] Davidson, op cit
[249] Cooper, J.C. *An Illustrated Encyclopaedia of Traditional Symbols.* London: Thames & Hudson Ltd. 1978, 178.
[250] Philpot, op cit ,14.

Tree spirits are also commonly believed in throughout Africa. The Ashanti reportedly believe that certain nature spirits are present that animate trees, stones and other "inanimate" objects as well as animals, rivers and charms. The powers of these spirits are great and respected. John Mbiti reports in his book *African Religions and Philosophy* of an incident that took place in Ghana in the 1960's. During the construction of a new harbor at Tema, equipment was repeatedly stolen and a company investigator, and Englishman, was sent to look into it. After his investigation was over one of the European supervisors mentioned to him that a lone tree was causing him a great deal of trouble. All the other trees in the area had been cleared but this one, which was relatively small, remained as all the heavy equipment stalled when approaching the tree. One of the African foremen said that the tree was magic and could not be removed unless the tree spirit could be persuaded to move on to another tree. A shaman was called in who sacrificed three sheep and poured three bottled of gin onto the roots of the tree as an offering. Evidently, the ritual worked as the machinery could be started. However, a few of the workers simply walked to the tree and were able to pull it up out of the earth. [251]

The Gods of Vegetation, discussed in another chapter, were all originally tree spirits who gave the gift of agriculture to humankind as well as learning, arts, and the other things that create civilization. They were also closely connected with death and the underworld.

---

[251] Mbiti op cit ,255.

The sycamore fig tree located in many desert areas of Egypt is said to be inhabited by goddesses. "These goddesses or spirits", Porteous noted, "sometimes manifest themselves, and…the head, or even the whole body, would emerge from the trunk of the tree, after a time re-entering it, being reabsorbed, or, as the Egyptian expression has it, the trunk *ate* it again." [252] The goddesses said to reside in the sycamore are Hathor (given the epithet "Lady of the Sycamore"), Nut, Selkit, and Isis. While certain male gods were also associated with trees, such as Osiris with the willow, Horus with the acacia and Wepwawet with the tamarisk), only these few goddesses were so closely associated with sacred trees. Like the carvings of females rising from vegetation found in contemporary architecture, these goddesses were most often shown as a "composite of the upper body of the goddess rising from the trunk at the center of a tree." [253] In the Egyptian world, the maternal deities were the tree goddesses, offering food to the deceased or, in the case of a mural in the tomb of Tuthmosis III, nursed by Isis in the form of a sycamore tree.

Dryads, or tree goddesses in India, are often depicted giving the trunk of a tree a little kick. The reason for this, according to Heinrich Zimmer, is found in a formula derived "from a ritual of fecundation. According to an ageless belief, nature requires to be stimulated by man; the procreative forces have to be aroused, by magic means, from semi-

---

[252] Porteous, op cit, 164.
[253] Wilkinson, Richard H. *The Complete Gods and Goddesses of Ancient Egypt.* London: Thames & Hudson Ltd. 2003, 169.

dormancy." [254] This ritual formula continues to be used in contemporary Indian culture. Zimmer adds, "There is in India a certain tree (*aśoka*) which is supposed not to put forth blossoms unless touched and kicked by a girl or young woman. Girls and young women," Zimmer wrote, "are regarded as human embodiments of the maternal energy of nature. They are diminutive doubles of the Great Mother of all life, vessels of fertility, life in full sap, potential sources of new offspring. By touching and kicking the tree they transfer into it their potency, and enable it to bring forth blossom and fruit."[255]

The Persians as well, according to J.H. Philpot, "venerated trees as the dwelling-place of the deity, as the haunts of good and evil spirits, and as the habitations in which the souls of heroes and the virtuous dead continued their existence." [256]

In ancient Crete, the Great Mother goddess was also known as the Lady of Trees and Doves—representing birth and fertility. In her early form the Great Mother of Crete, the Earth Mother, was rather vague—she was an ancient Neolithic goddess. In time, she became Demeter, goddess of animals, crops and forests. [257]

---

[254] Zimmer, Heinrich. *Myths and Symbols in Indian Art and Civilization.* Edited by Joseph Campbell. Princeton: Princeton University Press 1946, 69.

[255] Ibid.

[256] Philpot, Mrs. J.H. *The Sacred Tree in Religion and Myth.* Mineola: Dover Publications, Inc. 2004, 13 (A reprint of the 1897 edition published by Macmillan and Co. Ltd, London and New York)

[257] Mackenzie, Donald A. *Crete & Pre-Hellenic Myths and Legends.* London: Senate 1995, 175 (A reprint of the 1917 publication by the Gresham Publishing Company, London)

The gods and goddesses also lived within the trees of old Hawaii. The goddess of the ohia-lehua forest is one of these. The flower of the ohia tree is considered sacred and to pick it is forbidden unless proper invocations are said. One of the sacred ohia trees located in a cave of the god Ku-ka-ohia-laka is regarded as the body of this forefather-god. [258] The Hawaiian wind god, Makani-keoe, is another tree deity. Also known as a "love god", he is able to transform himself into a tree at will. An amulet made from such a tree is a powerful love charm but causes visions and voices to be heard by the one who obtains it.

Sacred groves in Germany were the homes of the gods as well. At Romove, the chief sacred grove, a holy oak figured in religious ceremonies and images of the gods were placed in its trunk. The Prussians who remained Pagan long after the rest of Germany had converted to Christianity used these groves into the 16th century. Davidson notes "writers who visited them described sacred woods in which they made sacrifices and sacred springs which Christians were not allowed to approach." [259] The god worshipped in the Prussian groves was Perkuno—the thunder god. It is believed that the word "Perkuno" is related to the Latin "quercus" meaning oak. Sacred groves were still utilized in Estonia into the 18th century as well. Every Dying God, such as Osiris, Adonis, Attis, Dionysus and Jesus, died on a tree. Mediaeval Christian carvings of the Tree of the Living and the

[258] Beckwith, Martha. *Hawaiian Mythology*. Honolulu: University of Hawaii Press1970, 16-17 (A reprint of the 1940 edition published by Yale University Press)
[259] Davidson, op cit

Dead (fruit of good and evil on opposite sides) depict Jesus as the trunk of the tree. [260]

Gautama Buddha is said to have been a tree-spirit "no less than forty-three times" in past incarnations. [261]

The Fate of Nature

It was only in November, 1997 that a leader of a patriarchal religion, Bartholomew I, head of the Greek Orthodox Church, stated that the "degradation of nature is a sin". No other leader of a Christian, Jewish, or Islamic body has ever made such a statement. To do so is revolutionary, even though Pagans and indigenous people around the world have held that belief since the beginning of time.

Most, if not all, of the worlds indigenous cultures view nature as a divine essence—the very essence of life. James G. Cowan, writing about the Australian aborigine said "they have studied nature, drawn their conclusions from it, and found it to be the embodiment of a profound metaphysical principal pertaining to all existence. For they have seen in nature much more than its visible beauty, fraternity and practical purpose as a provider. They have seen in it a symbol of an underlying reality which needs to be understood as sacred if true wisdom is to be attained." [262]

[260] Cooper, J.C. *An Illustrated Encyclopaedia of Traditional Symbols*. London: Thames & Hudson Ltd. 1978, 178.
[261] Philpot, Mrs. J.H. *The Sacred Tree in Religion and Myth*. Mineola: Dover Publications, Inc. 2004, 14.
[262] Cowan, James G. The Elements of the Aborigine Tradition. Shaftsbury: Element Books Limited 1992, 2.

Although the indigenous people of the non-Christian world viewed nature as the source of life, the real spiritual and sacred power of the world, early Christian missionaries condemned such thoughts and traditions saying that to continue the rituals, healings and worshipping at trees, stones and waterways "consecrate them to the devil." [263]

We find then that most "civilized" and "advanced" countries and societies have lost the sense of wonder and the knowledge that nature is much more than trees to be cleared for cattle and hills to be flattened for construction or oil to be pumped for increasingly larger vehicles. How did this occur? Humankind has always altered the environment and it would not be fair, nor accurate, to think otherwise. Prehistoric people were also guilty of eradicating species and whole forests. The Easter Islands is a prime example of misguided thought and poor planning decimating the landscape. Ronald Hutton Reminds us too that "the Iron Age Celts...may have had their holy stands of trees, but this did not stop them from clearing virtually all the large areas of forests spared by their predecessors...(and) under the pagan Roman Empire, the remaining woods were stripped from much of the North African coast, producing an ecological catastrophe...".[264]

However, these events were normally confined to certain, specific areas and were also used as military tactics. Since the advent of Christianity, this has become a worldwide catastrophe. For strange

---

[263] St. Eligius, AD 640 as quoted by Brian Bates in his article "Sacred Trees" in Resurgence Magazine #181, March/April 1997

[264] Hutton, Ronald. The Pagan Religions of the Ancient British Isles: Their Nature and Legacy. Oxford: Blackwell 1993, 253.

reasons Christianity, consumerism and big business seem to go hand in hand. Theologian Rosemary Radford Ruether wrote of the conflict in her book Gaia & God:

"One side of this tradition (of Christian asceticism), with its hostility to women, sexuality, and the body, and its contempt for the material world in favor of life after death, reinforces the patterns of neglect and flight from the earth. But asceticism can also be understood, not as rejection of the body and the earth, but rather as rejection of exploitation and excess, and thus as a return to egalitarian simple living in harmony with other humans and with nature." [265]

For the most part this asceticism is defined narrowly and is not eco-friendly. This is slowly changing with the works of Christian scholars such as Matthew Fox, Ruether and others but even now; most Christian/Catholic clergy and congregations are very resistant to looking upon the natural world as more than a hindrance to their journey to heaven or a temptation toward evil. Nature became evil and associated with witchcraft. Women were viewed as completely untrustworthy, evil and the essence of death and sin. "This ambivalence toward women", writes Ruether "was closely related to Christian ambivalence toward physical nature." [266]

The ambivalence toward women was also a result of the fear of women by the patriarchal leaders. This ambivalence was driven by the

---

[265] Ruether, Rosemary Radford. Gaia & God: An Ecofeminist Theology of Earth Healing. San Francisco: HarperSanFrancisco 1992, 188.
[266] Ibid,189.

fear of the Goddess religion and that a matriarchal society would once again become a dominant force around the world.

The negative attitudes expressed today towards women and nature in general are those same attitudes expressed since the advent of patriarchal religion of Biblical times. Sex and fertility are regarded as sinful, as evil temptations to be shunned, ignored and suppressed. Women are at the disposal of males. One of the ignominious questions of early theologians was "Do women have souls?"

For many conservative Christians, nature and all of her plant and animal children are soulless, there for the pure exploitation and dominance of man and regarded as habitats for evil. Eleventh century theologians Peter Abelard and Hidegard of Bingen both believed that demons occupied trees and that the devil existed within nature. An example of this is found in carvings located in St. Lazare church in Autun, France. Built in the twelfth century, one notable piece shows two demons hanging a soul from stalks of flowering vines. [267] There is no stewardship professed in most religions today as there was during the pre-historic Goddess era although there are signs that this may be changing—hopefully before it is too late. Those few societies that do still exist today that view nature as sacred and to be protected are regarded as "primitive".

These people, as all other indigenous cultures throughout time, "depended on being able to enter into the very psyche of the

---

[267] Kostof. Spiro. A History of Architecture: Settings and Ritual. Oxford: Oxford University Press 1985, 300.

environment". [268] "Our forefathers of fifteen hundred years ago," writes Brian Branston "lived not what we call 'close to nature' but actually involved with nature: they were not creatures apart, different from the birds, plants or animals, but fitted into the natural cycle of synthesis and disintegration which any kind of civilization always modifies....It is from the constant awareness of the living connection between man and the phenomenal world that the myths of our ancestors arise, that their gods are born." [269]

The residents of today's "advanced" societies are no longer able to do this wonderful thing, which has resulted in billions of people losing touch with their spirituality and ethical living on the earth.

---

[268] Bates, Brian. "Sacred Trees" in *Resurgence Magazine* #181, March/April 1997.
[269] Branston, Brian. The Lost Gods of England. New York: Oxford University Press 1974, 52-53.

Chapter Four
Lilith & Baal – First Casualties

There have been many gods and goddesses worshipped by humankind over the last several thousands of years and all of them have been changed from their original personalities and positions of importance to reflect only a dim image of what they once were.

In this chapter, we will examine two of these gods and delve into their origins and how they have been made into evil and base creatures. The first of these will be Lilith.

Lilith

Lilith was a bird goddess, shown in the Burney Plaque of Sumer from 2300 BCE, represented by the Great Owl. The plaque (see illustration on page 131) shows a seductive, winged woman with bird-taloned feet and wearing only the tiara that was worn by all of the ancient gods. She is also shown holding the ring and rod of power. Like other goddesses, she is shown accompanied by a pair of lions, upon which she stands.

The owls signify her wisdom as well as her nocturnal nature. Lilith, which means "screech owl" in Hebrew, was goddess of the Underworld, the Great Goddess of Death.

Lilith appears in the Sumerian epic of Gilgamesh. In Gilgamesh, the actual dethroning of Lilith is referred to. The Sumerian goddess

Inanna plants a huluppu tree, a willow that is sacred to the Ancient Mother goddess. Inanna plans to cut the tree and use the wood to create a throne (magical, of course) and a bed. What Inanna doesn't know is that Lilith has, in her owl form, created a home in the tree. At the base of the tree, a large serpent, also associated with Lilith, was protecting it. Nothing that Inanna could do would make the serpent move or Lilith to leave her house.

The myth tells the story:

"Inanna cared for the tree with her hand.

She settled the earth around the tree with her foot.

She wondered:

'How long will it be until I have a shining throne to sit upon?'

'How long will it be until I have a shining bed to lie upon?'

"The years passed; five years, then ten years.

The tree grew thick,

But its bark did not split.

Then a serpent who could not be charmed

Made its nest in the roots of the huluppu-tree.

The Anzu-bird set his young in the branches of the tree.

And the dark maid Lilith built her home in the trunk.

The young woman who loved to laugh wept.

How Inanna wept!

(Yet they would not leave her tree.)" [270]

---

[270] Wolkstein, Diane and Samuel Noah Kramer. *Inanna: Queen of Heaven and Earth.* New York: Harper & Row, Publishers 1983, 5-6.

In her distress Inanna turns to her hero-brother, Gilgamesh.

Gilgamesh "struck the serpent who could not be charmed.

"The Anzu-bird flew with his young to the mountains;

And Lilith smashed her home and flew to the wild, uninhabited

places." [271]

Lililth as carved on the Burney plaque, 1950 BCE.

This myth is interesting as it is told from the standpoint of a new goddess, Inanna, who has forced out a goddess far older, Lilith. Lilith's nude form, according to Johnson, "creates an identification with the Naked Goddess, suggesting a state of nature. However powerful she

---

[271] Ibid., 9.

may have been in early Sumerian times, she is greatly diminished in the Old Testament, where she appears as temptress and she-demon rather than the great Goddess of Death." [272]

The fact that Lilith held the ring and rod of power on a Sumerian tablet indicates that at one time she was considered a very powerful deity.

While what is known about Lilith is at best sketchy, many scholars believe that she brought the knowledge of agriculture to humankind. Her fiercely independent nature resulted in her demonization. In Hebrew lore Lilith was Adam's first wife (or mother). Because she refused to lie beneath Adam, [273] demanding equality, she left him and found a life in the desert away from him. God sent three angels after her where they found her near the Red Sea, living with evil spirits. She refused to return to Adam, instead living in the wild and giving birth to more than a hundred demons each day. God's punishment was to kill 100 of her offspring each day she remained apart from Adam. According to Talmudic texts from the 4th and 13th centuries CE, Lilith was made by god from filth and sediment rather then the pure dust that he created Adam from. This is the basis for much of the denigration of the female.

Lilith became the original succubus, seducing men in their sleep and was believed responsible for strangling infants soon after birth. In

---

[272] Johnson, Buffie. *Lady of the Beasts: The Goddess and her sacred animals.* Rochester: Inner Traditions 1994, 83.
[273] According to legend, the children of Lilith and Adam were demons.

fact Lilith may have been the first Mother Goddess. In an effective attempt to reduce the Mother Goddess's important role she became demonized, the cause of original sin. Jean Markale believes that the shift from goddess to god began when people realized that men had a role in procreation. Until that time women created children in a mysterious and obviously divine way—without the need of the male.

"Beginning from when the individual male is established as indispensable procreator," write Markale, "revealing the existence of a paternal lineage, it became important to hide the feminine genitals, too closely linked to the liturgies in honor of the Great Goddess, the idealized image of all women. Under these conditions, it was natural that Mosaism—and other theologies of the ancient world as well—should oppose what they called idolatry, that is, all the earlier forms of worship, notably the sexual forms, almost exclusively the prerogative of women." [274]

Lilith was a casualty of the early struggles between the father god and the mother goddess. Markale summarizes her defeat: "As soon as the cult of Yahweh triumphed, the Goddess of the Beginnings was reduced to her simplest form, and Lilith of the rabbinical tradition, consigned to darkness." [275] Lilith was, according to folklorist Howard Schwartz, the original witch and her legends "gave birth to an elaborate

---

[274] Markale, Jean. *The Great Goddess.* Rochester: Inner Traditions 1999, 10.
[275] Ibid., 49.

Jewish demonology." [276] It was Lilith's legend that gave birth to the vampire.

Markale believes that Lilith survived the persecution—becoming the Black Virgin found throughout the Old World.

Baal

Baal was not so despised or hunted as the goddess in Biblical society. The reasons for this are fairly simple, the goddess was the most powerful of deities controlling food, fertility and sexuality among other things. Baal, on the other hand, was not dissimilar to Yahweh. "The image of Yahweh, in the eyes of the common people," wrote Raphael Patai, "did not differ greatly from that of Baal or the other Canaanite male gods....The worship of Yahweh thus easily merged into, complimented, or supplanted that of the Canaanite male gods." [277]

Baal was a usurper as well, replacing the supreme Ugaritic-Canaanite god El and taking his consort, Ashera. We have already discussed Ashera and will discuss her again. Baal's position in the pantheon of gods was as "exalted lord of the earth" whose main task was to control fertility and renew vegetation. [278]

Baal was also called "Rider of the Cloud" and was a storm god. He was also represented by the bull as a symbol of fertility. It should not

[276] Schwartz, Howard. *Lilith's Cave*. Oxford: Oxford University Press 1988, 8.

[277] Patai, Raphael. *The Hebrew Goddess*. New York: Avon Books 1978, 12.

[278] Skinner, Fred Gladstone. *Myths and Legends of the Ancient Near East*. New York: Barnes & Noble Books 1993, 110.

be assumed that Baal was a patriarchal god, taking the goddesses tradition role in fertility and renewal. Baal was an androgenous god. His worshipped were said to invoke him as: "Hear us, Baal! Whether thou be god or a goddess." [279] For each of the masculine forms of his name, a corresponding female form was also used.

Baal and Yahweh are very similar in their personalities. Archaeologist John Romer notes "Both Ugarit's great God Baal and Jehovah 'mount to the clouds' in their respective chariots, both 'utter voice' in thunder and storm, and both stand 'at the head of the assembly of gods.'"[280]

In fact, Romer states that the ancient Jewish sacred liturgy, "both of its architecture and of its written word," originated in Bronze Age Canaan. [281]

Skinner notes that the "Hebrews, although formally opposed to the religion of Canaan, actually adopted many of its features, particularly such cultic aspects as the fertility cult of the mother goddess, the life-death myth in agriculture, and the practice of temple prostitution." [282] They also embraced Baal. Professor John Gray, Lecturer in Hebrew and Biblical Criticism at Aberdeen University, wrote "The Ras Shamra Texts now prove conclusively that the Canaanite Baal was Hadad, the god manifest in the rains and thunder of autumn and winter and

[279] Inman, Thomas. *Ancient Pagan and Modern Christian Symbolism*. New York: Cosimo Classics 2005, 119.
[280] Romer, John. *Testament: The Bible and History*. Old Saybrook: Konecky & Konecky 1988, 79.
[281] Ibid.
[282] Skinner, op cit., 113.

secondarily in the vegetation which they promoted." [283] In other words, Baal was a nature god.

The Hebrew leadership, however, could not abide with two gods of equal stature. Obviously, Baal had to go.

According to the Biblical account, the prophet Elijah confronted King Ahab, telling Ahab that he had "forsaken the commandments of the Lord, and thou hast followed Baalim." [284]

To prove that Yahweh was greater than Baal, Elijah had Ahab gather the 450 priests of Baal together at Mt Carmel. When they had gathered, Elijah told the priests of Baal to choose one of two bullocks and to kill it and to cut it into pieces. Then they were to place the meat on wood but not to light it. Likewise, Elijah did the same. They were then to call upon Baal to set the wood on fire. As they did this they were met with silence. They continued to call upon Baal for two days suffering the mocking of Elijah: "...either he is talking, or he is pursuing, or he is on a journey, or peradventure he sleepeth..." [285]

Then it was Elijah's turn. He gathered twelve stones, made an altar with a trench around it and told his followers to pour three barrels of water over the wood and meat. The water ran down and filled the trench. He then called on god to send fire from heaven to consume the

---

[283] Gray, John. *Archaeology and the Old Testament World.* Edinburgh: Thomas Nelson and Sons LTD. 1962, 17.
[284] 1 Kings 18:18. Note, "Baalim" is plural for Baal, which simply means "lord."
[285] 1 Kings 18: 27.

wood. This was done. Elijah then bound the 450 priests of Baal and took them to a brook called Kishon were they were slaughtered.

We have to wonder, was that truly water that was poured over the altar or, perhaps, a flammable liquid perhaps unknown to the priests? Did Elijah perform a bit of magical slight of hand to destroy the followers of a rival god?

Christian theology maintains the myth of the evil of Baal and the other gods even though Yahweh was more than likely an identical god fashioned into a useable force by the Hebrew priests.

The 1965 edition of Halley's Bible Handbook speaks eloquently, but falsely, of the Canaanite religion:

"The worship of Baal, Ashtoreth, and the other Canaanite gods consisted in the most extravagant orgies, their temples were centers of vice." [286]

Official evangelical Christian theology claims that "Prophets of Baal and Ashtoreth were official murderers of little children," [287] even though the Bible itself records the slaughter of men, women and "little ones" by the Hebrews as they took the region by force—not once but time and again. Like all victors, the Hebrew monotheists rewrote many portions of the Bible to fit their views and the "history" they desired.

After the initial victory of the Hebrews in Canaan Yahweh was not forced upon the populace but was only proposed to be the chief god

---

[286] Halley, Henry. *Halley's Bible Handbook*. Grand Rapids: Zondervan Publishing House 1965, 166.
[287] Ibid, 198.

of Israel. "In the beginning," wrote professor Rodney Stark, "this sect movement seems not to have advocated strict monotheism, but merely to have proposed that although there were other Gods, Israelites should worship Yahweh only. That is, Yahweh was deemed the national God to whom Israel owed exclusive allegiance..."[288]

The conflict raged however until King Hezekiah was finally able to significantly reduce the number of supporters of Baal between 715 – 687 BCE.

---

[288] Stark, Rodney. *Discovering God: The Origins of the Great Religions and the Evolution of Belief.* New York: HarperCollins 2007, 183.

Chapter Five
Mithras – Christianity's Rival

We have briefly discussed Mithras but a more thorough examination needs to be made since the religion centered around this saviour-god was such a force in ancient times. Scholar Ernest Renan is reported to have said, "If the growth of Christianity had been halted by some mortal illness, the world would have become Mithraic."[289]

Mithras is an ancient god that some believe to have been a Sun god at one time. In fact, Elworthy writes, "It is the general opinion that the Sun, Serapis, Mithras, Dis, Typhon, Attis, Ammon, and Adonis were one and the same god."[290]

Mithras, an Indo-Iranian god dating from at least the Bronze Age, was worshipped wherever Persian influence dominated in the world. His name means "the middle one" perhaps referencing his role in treaties and alliances, "friend" and "contract".

The Mithraic religion pretty much followed the Roman soldier as they traversed the known world, the Roman soldier was one of Mithra's converts as were many of the Roman merchants and officials.

---

[289] As quoted by Walter Burkert in *Ancient Mystery Cults*. Cambridge: Harvard University Press 1987, 3.
[290] Elworthy, Frederick Thomas. *The Evil Eye: The Classic Account of an Ancient Superstition*. Mineola: Dover Publications 2004, 353fn. (A reprint of the 1895 edition published by John Murray, London)

One of the "Mystery Religions," Mithraism was practiced in subterranean caves were initiations were undertaken along with sacrificial meals.

There are many similarities between Mithraic theology and the later Christianity. Mithra was the first god who rewarded true penance, he would punish those who sin, usually with an illness, but he also forgave. [291]

"Mithras was a god of light, engaged in a constant struggle with Ariman, the evil prince of darkness." [292] Mithra was a creator god and images of him slaying the bull represent blood being the source of life. Mithraism was a male dominant religion, originating among the Aryan tribes that became the Indo-Europeans. There are many puzzles about this mystery religion, perhaps rightfully so. A name for the followers was never coined except by others. We know that the small groups of worshippers that converged in the caves for ritual, feasting and initiation must have had a feeling of togetherness but, according to Burkert, "the language is circumstantial and individualistic." [293]

Mithraism, according to James, "provided a link between a sacramental religion and morality." [294] Mithraic theology motivated its followers to live a good life. Mithras was "the mediator between the

---

[291] Cooper, D. Jason. *Mithras: Mysteries and Initiation Rediscovered.* York Beach: Samuel Weiser, Inc. 1996, 4.
[292] *Encyclopedia of Ancient Myths and Cultures.* London: Quantum Publishing Ltd. 2003, 701.
[293] Burkert, op cit., 47.
[294] James, E.O. *The Ancient Gods.* Edison: Castle Books 2004, 317.

celestial powers and the human race."[295] Mithra was eternally involved in the struggle of light and darkness, goodness and evil. His followers were given tools through their teachings on their own cosmic struggle to not only fight successfully in battle but to be successful in controlling their temptations and passions as human beings.

Mithras' origins lay in the Vedic god of light, Mitra and they are both associated with fire. In fact, Zoroaster is thought to have been closely tied to Mithraism and, as such, continues the Mithraic tradition even today in parts of Iran where Temples of Fire continue to exist, the eternal flames attended to by dedicated followers.

The failure of Mithraism, according to some scholars, is that while it offered hope in defeating ones personal evils it did not promise an afterlife, which, we know, Christianity does. Mithraism, though, did not demand exclusivity but was companionable with any other religion. This was a true difference between it and Christianity and Judaism, which demanded unequivocal and obedient worship. It would have been interesting to see the world take shape under Mithraism if Constantine had not endorsed Christianity but had embraced Mithras as most of his military and officials had already done. It may be that these same scholars would be writing something similar about Christianity being a cult of tombs and death—not of eternal life.

---

[295] Ibid., 318.

Chapter Six
The Transition

For thousands of years humankind stood in awe of nature—both of its beauty, its ability to renew itself and in the power of its animals and storms. Over time, this reverence transferred to the Earth Goddess, which assumed a more human form although always intimately linked to the animal world and the very geography of the planet.

A very few thousands of years ago things changed. The change was sudden, violent and has continued into our own time.

The Goddess Cult

To understand the nature of the change we must first examine the "cult" of the Mother Goddess. I need to explain that the use of the word "cult" is prescribed by current academic convention. Most dominating religions or cultures will prescribe the term "cult" to any religion not of their own even though such a "cult" was as valid a religion as any we have today—with probably more adherents!

Before politics, before organized theocracies and kingdoms, before the Biblical history, existed a religious tradition based upon female deities. "...the Earth-goddess was conceived as the generative power in nature as a whole," wrote E.O. James, "and so she became responsible for the periodic renewal of life in the spring after the blight of winter or the summer drought. She therefore assumed the form of a many-sided goddess, both mother and bride..." [296]

Many Earth-Mother figurines have been discovered over the years pre-dating by thousands of years any of today's religions. Some of these figurines have been dated to 25,000 BCE, such as one found at Laussel, Dordogne, France which has been interpreted to be "both the sacred female and sacred nature." [297] This particular figure was carved on a cave opening in such a manner that the rising sun first cast its rays on the figure before alighting on the cave opening.

Thousands of years later, around 7000 BCE, similar figures were made in abundance at Çatal Hüyük, an important sacred city located in Anatolia, in today's Turkey. Many of the goddesses made here show her in association with lions and, in fact, many show the goddess with a cat-like form. Çatal Hüyük was a "city of shrines" that attest to a complex society based on goddess worship, agriculture and peace. There is substantial evidence that this was a matriarchal society where "religious practice was intimate, personal, integrated into rhythms of ordinary life." [298] This was truly an ancient utopia with a goddess represented by the leopard but intimately linked to the production of grain and the arts.

Other goddess centers existed in other parts of the world at this time as well. A goddess centered culture was created by the hunting

[296] James, E.O. *The Ancient Gods*. Edison: Castle Books 2004, 77-78.
[297] Gadon, Elinor W. *The Once & Future Goddess*. San Francisco: Harper & Row 1989, 14.
[298] Ibid., 36.

and fishing people of Lepinski Vir in the Danube River Basin around 6500 BCE. Large river rocks were shaped into hybrid creatures, half fish and half human, some with breasts, which appear to have represented "a primeval creator or a mythical ancestress." [299]

It is interesting to note that the fish was an ancient symbol of the goddess—universally found—which also became the symbol of the Christian savior.

Other goddess centers existed at Sabatnovka, Moldavia, dating to 5000 BCE. Altars with goddess figurines have been found here, on one altar alone sixteen figures were found all seated on horn-back stools. One of the figures was made holding a baby snake.

The goddess tradition was flourishing at Knossos 1500 years later. The Goddess of Knossos was a goddess of the beasts. She is shown on carving, signets and paintings with lions, bulls, griffins, doves and sphinxes. She is also associated with sacral horns and the sacred tree pillar—a symbol of the World Tree. It is probably the fabulous culture of Knossos that is responsible for the spread of the goddess tradition into other Mediterranean lands such as Sparta, Syria, Cyprus, Palestine and Israel.

The Queen of Heaven

When the Hebrews entered Palestine and Canaan, they were met with as much philosophical and religious resistance as military. Far from walking into an unoccupied Land of Milk and Honey, the

---

[299] Gadon, op cit.,43.

Hebrews arrived to forcefully take the land away and to forcefully install their religion. As in many instances of invasion the local people, their customs and beliefs were subject to attack and only those that acquiesced survived.

Ancient Canaan and the other immediate countries around Canaan worshipped two deities, on, El, also called Asher, and the other Asherah. El was the sun god, later replaced by Baal, and Asherah the goddess of the moon. To the Canaanites Asherah was the consort to El and both were instrumental in keeping the world fertile. The Hebrew incursion into Canaan was terrible, violent and sweeping. The Bible itself gives the telling evidence of the wonton disregard for property and life that the Hebrews disposed of in order to obtain the land. After God supposedly demanded Moses to sacrifice a large number of animals to him, the Hebrews "slew all the males," all of the kings that stood in their way, and then they "took all the women of Midian captives, and their little ones, and took the spoil of all their cattle, and all their flocks, and all their goods. And the burnt all their cities wherein their dwelt, and all their castles, with fire." [300]

The spoils of war were divided between the warriors and the rest of the Hebrews. Moreover, what booty it was! Six-hundred seventy thousand sheep, over one thousand asses and thirty-two thousand girls "that had not known man by lying with him." [301]

---

[300] **Numbers 31: 8-10**
[301] **Numbers 31: 35**

The slaughter did not end with the Midianites but continued across the land. City after city, kingdom after kingdom, were destroyed to the very last man as the Hebrews consumed the land in the name of the Lord. "And we took all his cities (the king of Heshbon) at that time, and utterly destroyed the men, and the women, and the little ones, of every city, we left none to remain." [302] Jericho is another example of Hebrew barbarity. Again, the Hebrew Yahweh gave the cities and land of the original inhabitants to the Hebrews and ordered Joshua to take it. According to Joshua 6: 21, "And they utterly destroyed all that was in the city, both man and woman, young and old, and ox, the sheep, and ass, with the edge of the sword." Likewise, the Hebrews attempted to wipe out any remnant of the religion of these people. Goddess worship was one important aspect of this cultural "sanitation."

The primary religion of Canaan and the surrounding area was that of goddess worship. While Ashera was regarded as a consort to the male god, El she was of primary importance to the people of this area. In Jeremiah 44: 2 we find god boasting of the destruction that was brought about in his name, "Ye have seen all the evil that I have brought upon Jerusalem, and upon all the cities of Judah; and, behold, this day they are a desolation, and no man dwelleth therein." But the destruction wasn't over yet.

Supposedly god was furious, or rather the warrior-priests speaking for god, that the inhabitants of the lands of Egypt to Judah continued

---

[302] Deuteronomy 3: 34

to worship Ashera. God's warning is all too clear: "they shall die, from the least even unto the greatest, by the sword and by the famine: and they shall be an exercation, and an astonishment, and a curse, and a reproach. For I shall punish them...as I have punished Jerusalem, by the sword, by the famine, and by the pestilence."

Jeremiah was sent by the Hebrew god to convince the people that they must throw away their goddess and god or face the wrath of Yahweh. The response was:

"As for the word that thou hast spoken unto us in the name of the Lord, we will not hearken unto thee.

"But we will certainly do whatsoever thing goeth forth out of our own mouth, to burn incense unto the queen of heaven, and to pour out drink offerings unto her, as we have done, we, and our fathers, our kings, and our princes, in the cities of Judah, and in the streets of Jerusalem: for then we had plenty of victuals, and we were well, and saw no evil.

"But since we left off to burn incense to the queen of heaven, and to pour out drink offerings unto her, we have wanted all things, and have been consumed by the sword and by famine."[303]

At first, the Hebrews attempted to pacify the population by "allowing" Asahera to be recognized as the consort of Yahweh. As writer Alexander Waugh notes, "...when El was usurped by the Jewish

---

[303] Jeremiah, 44: 17-18

Yahweh who became the one and only god of all the universe, the goddess Asherah was, for a while at least, dragged along to be his consort." [304]

During this time, the Hebrews actually embraced Ashera as the bride of Yahweh. For over three hundred years standing stones, representatives of Ashera, stood in the temple in Jerusalem. The worship of Ashera "continued in spite of the antipolythestic teachings of the prophets and later Biblical redactors," writes historian Fred Gladstone Skinner. "Temples to Yahweh and Ashtoreth existed side by side. The veneration of Ashera is mentioned forty times in the Old Testament. It was introduced into the cultus of the royal household by Solomon…and became a part of temple ritual." [305] Around 700 BCE, the priests finally had the stones removed and destroyed—along with the brazen serpent that Moses reportedly placed in the Ark of the Covenant. It was during this period of time that priests of the male god Yahweh along with the development of bronze weapons and the massive incursions of war-like patriarchal tribes from the steppes pushed into the areas previously dominated by the goddess cultures and wiped them out. Women were no longer viewed as equals but were reduced to items of property, their views and values ignored. Women became sacrificial objects to be dominated and used.

---

[304] Waugh, Alexander. *God.* New York: St. Martin's Press 2002, 35.
[305] Skinner, Fred Gladstone. *Myths and Legends of the Ancient Near East.* New York: Barnes & Noble Books 1993, 111.

Referred to as the "Kurgan incursion," this cultural expansion resulted when a "warlike pastoral society, highly mobile…which employed both wagons drawn by oxen and rode horses…burst in on later Neolithic or Eneolithic cultures of Eastern and Central Europe and brought about a thorough transformation of European society." [306]

Originating in the Volga-Ural area of Eastern Europe, this horde of patriarchal warriors spread throughout Europe and south into Mesopotamia, India, Iran and Central Asia. Because of their tradition of raising livestock rather than agriculture, their incursion changed the entire economic dynamic of the areas under their domination and also began to change the religious and political structures as cattle breeding replaced grain and agriculture. We know that agricultural communities were goddess based and the cattle breeders were traditionally father-god based.

The effects of the incursion were dramatic. Populations were widely displaced, pottery was pushed out, painted ware disappears, the copper industry of the Balkans collapses and is replaced by bronze, and the matrifocal societies which had predominated in these areas with their thousands of goddess figurines disappears "under the Kurgan warriors whose religious attention was more attracted to warlike sky-gods and sun worship." [307]

---

[306] Mallory, J.P. *In Search of the Indo-Europeans: Language, Archaeology and Myth*. New York: Thames and Hudson 1989, 183
[307] Ibid., 184.

While a direct link between the Indo-European Kurgans and the Semitic peoples has not been made, their similar migratory herding societies obviously produced many of the same socio-political structures, religions and desires to obtain as much land for the herds as possible. It is probable that the ancient Hebrews and the Kurgans had intermingled producing a warlike, nomadic society focusing on expansion and domination.

In those societies where the goddess continued to be worshipped, she was reduced to secondary status as the wife or mother of the chief male gods, the gods of war and thunder. Over time, goddesses like Athena and Diana became patronesses of war and battle.

Eventually the old order under the goddess became a thing of myth—the Golden Age of peace and harmony, of technological and artistic advancement never before seen and now lost forever.

Attacks on ancient religion continued as Christianity took hold with pagan temples, images, books and other artifacts destroyed and pagan adherents slaughtered. Merlin Stone notes that the Old Testament "does not even have a word for 'Goddess.'" But, she points out, the Koran makes it perfectly clear what Islamic and Judeo-Christian attitudes were: "Allah will not tolerate idolatry...the pagans pray to females." [308]

---

[308] Stone, Merlin. *When God was a Woman*. New York: Barnes & Noble Books 1993, xviii.

It is interesting that religions predicated on peace, charity and tolerance has their beginnings in an aggressive, extremely violent and intolerant tradition.

Chapter Seven
God of War

As shown, the Biblical Jehovah was not a god of peace but one that advocated war and plunder. We know, of course, that the Hebrew priests were calling the shots. Through them commands for exploitation and war were given for land, women, gold and livestock. Strangely enough, the Bible is quite honest in their deeds and motives.

When the Hebrews entered Canaan, they were instructed to send spies out to survey the land to see if it was worth taking. The spies returned, reporting, "We came unto the land whither thou sentest us, and surely it floweth with milk and honey…" After some debate, Caleb says "Let us go up at once, and possess it; for we are well able to overcome it." [309]

With the Hebrew incursion in Canaan and the subsequent barbarian invasions through Old Europe and the Middle East a rapid and profound change in the makeup of the world occurred—a change that we are still dealing with today.

Warfare became a way of life. It became even more savage and relentless than it ever had been. "God" became absolutely male, even though, as Waugh wrote, he was "a deity without a phallus." [310]

---

[309] Numbers 13:27-30
[310] Waugh, Alexander. *God.* New York: St. Martin's Press 2002, 35.

"The picture that emerges from our revised reading of the fragmentary archaeological evidence," wrote Elinor Gadon, "is of a popular polytheism that was violently opposed by a jealous priesthood and proselytizing prophets." [311]

The Hebrew displacement of indigenous religion was not a quick one, however. It took hundreds of years to finally force the surrounding tribes and people into submission—at a cost of untold lives of those being dominated. Like the assimilation of Ashera, the male god Baal was also assimilated into Hebrew religion—for a time.

"The early cult of the Israelites was adapted from Canaanite practice," notes Gadon, "with its sacrificial system, ritual objects, and images and included both the worship of the Goddess and sacred prostitution." [312]

It also included the Canaanite god Baal who was regarded as the god of the land while Yahweh was the sky-god. For a considerable time after the Hebrews established their presence in Canaan, they actually abandoned Yahweh and worshipped Baal and Ashera. Samuel undertook a cleansing operation however, destroying images of the Old Gods with continuous attacks on the goddess worshippers. These attacks lasted for five hundred years.

In the seventh century BCE the Hebrew priests convinced King Josiah to make a concerted armed attack on the holy places of Ashera

---

[311] Gadon, Elinor W. *The Once and Future Goddess*. San Francisco: Harper & Row, Publishers 1989, 180.
[312] Ibid., 181.

and Baal: "Ye shall utterly destroy all the places wherein the nations...served their gods, upon the high mountains, and upon the hills, and under every green tree:

"And ye shall overthrow their altars, and break their pillars, and burn their groves with fire; and ye shall hew down the graven images of their gods, and destroy the names of them out of that place." [313]

Josiah also ordered the extermination of all non-Hebrew peoples living in Canaan and prohibited intermarriage with them in the surrounding areas. Some have compared the Hebrew religion to "a male fertility cult" which took the act of creation away from the female goddess and transferred it solely to the male god.

"The gods of the Semites dwelt in clouds and on mountain tops," says Anne Baring and Jules Cashford, "and hurled thunderbolts like the gods of the Aryans. But they had more the character of tribal gods, each protective of a specific tribal group and, later, of a city." [314] Both the Semites and the Aryans, as invaders, introduced the concept of light and dark, good and evil as opposites.

Prior to this, these opposites were considered part of the whole, not as a polarity but as a duality. Guilt, death and futility were the overriding messages of the invaders, which drastically altered the world view of life and existence. Death as a violent end became the norm

---

[313] Deuteronomy 12: 2-3.
[314] Baring, Anne and Jules Cashford. *The Myth of the Goddess: Evolution of An Image.* London: Arkana/Penguin Books 1993, 157

rather than the exception. The earth became a playground for destruction and subjugation. Nature was only to be controlled, exploited and dominated, not nourished. The effects of these attitudes are still felt today with the constant wars for oil, the degradation of habitat and the struggle, often violent and terrible, between faiths that, allegedly, worship the same god.

As history has shown, it was not Baal or the other gods of ancient people that manifested themselves in aggressive and warlike acts but the god of the Hebrews. A god later embraced by those who were to become Christians and Muslims as well.

The belief in One God, supreme over all, in itself diminishes tolerance for others of different beliefs. But beliefs are only second in importance when it comes to war and exploitation. One's beliefs are often twisted to fit the "cause" of conflict and are precluded from resolving the conflict.

During the 4th century, the great pagan scholar and scientist Hypatia was hacked to death by Christian monks "because she was an iniquitous female who had presumed, against God's commandments, to teach men." [315]

A series of Church laws and acts of violence finally resulted in the desired end. Such acts and attitudes have been perpetuated since. The following illustrates these historic events:

---

[315] Ellerbe, Hellen. *The Dark Side of Christian History.* Orlando: Morningstar and Lark 1995, 8.

- 319 CE – Law passed by Constantine excusing the clergy from paying taxes and serving in the military

- 355 CE – Bishops exempt from being tried in secular courts

- 380 CE – Theodosius passes decree that everyone shall believe in one deity and that the name "Catholic Christians" shall be embraced, all others are considered demented and insane

- 380 CE – Law passed to make it illegal to disagree with the Church

- 388 CE – Public discussions of religion forbade

- 391 CE – Library of Alexandria burned by Christians, resulting in the loss of over 700,000 ancient texts. Education of anyone outside the Church structure ends.

- 392 CE – Pagan religion and practices outlawed

- 398 CE – Fourth Council of Carthage forbids Bishops from reading any book by "gentiles"

- 410 CE – Assembly by persons to practice pagan worship punished by "exile and blood"

- 435 CE – Only Christianity and Judaism permitted, all others considered heretics and threatened with death

- 540 CE – Bubonic plague strikes Byzantium, killing a reported 10,000 persons each day. The Church claims that the plague is an act of God and a punishment for the sin of disobeying Church authority.

- 553 CE – Belief in reincarnation and the pre-existence of the soul outlawed

- Technology disappears, disease runs rampant as toilets and indoor plumbing no longer used, medicine and medical techniques forbidden by the Church, replaced by bleeding

- 1099 CE – Both Muslims and Jews massacred at Jerusalem. "It was a just and marvelous judgment of God," wrote chronicler Raymond of Aguilers, "that this place should be filled with the blood of unbelievers."

- 1204 CE – Pope Innocent III launched a crusade against Constantinople for failing to submit to Church rule

- 1208 CE – Pope Innocent III launches a crusade against the Cathars, a religious group in southern France which held a diverse religious view and allowed women to be priests, an estimated one million people are slaughtered

- 1210 – 1215 CE – The teaching of Aristotle's works restricted

- 1219 CE – The Pope forbids priests from studying Roman law and outlaws its study at the University of Paris

- 1231 CE – Pope Gregory IX establishes the Inquisition, Papal edict requires heretics to be burned to death

- 1252 CE – Pope Innocent IV sanctions the use of torture to obtain confessions, this a legal option of the Church until 1917

- 1272 CE – Any theological discussion forbidden

- 1275 CE – The Pope excommunicates Florence when they refuse to pay tribute

- 1302 CE – Pope Boniface passes a decree that rules "it is altogether necessary to salvation for every human creature to be subject to the Roman pontiff"

- 1326 CE – Decree passed that those who believed that Jesus and his disciples owned no property are heretical

- 1353 CE – Turks take Gallipoli, entering Europe

- 1377 CE – Cessna, Italy laid waste with thousands slaughtered for refusal to pay tribute to the Church by Robert of Geneva who was to become Clement VII in 1378 CE.

- 1389 CE – Turks reach the Danube in their expansion into Europe

- 1391 CE – The Archdeacon of Seville launches a "Holy War against the Jews". By 1492, the Spanish inquisition requires Jews to convert to Christianity or suffer expulsion from Spain.

- 1484 CE – Pope Innocent VIII authorizes the persecution of witches

- 1484 CE – Pope Innocent VIII orders the slaughter of pet cats as they could be witches familiars

- 1488 CE – It becomes heresy to not believe in witchcraft

- 1492 CE – Columbus vows to "convert the heathen Indians to our Holy faith"

- 1493 CE – War is justified against any Native American in South America who refused to adhere to Christianity

- 1517 CE – Martin Luther nails his 95 theses to the door of his church, creating the Protestant Reformation

- 1525 CE – Martin Luther supports the brutal suppression of the Peasants War

- 1531 CE – Martin Luther affirms the Wittenberg edict sanctioning the execution of Anabaptists

- 1533 CE – Martin Luther writes that girls begin to talk and walk before boys "because weeds always grow more quickly than good crops"

- 1570 CE – The Inquisition is established in Peru and Mexico to force the conversion of the indigenous races to Christianity. Those who refused were burned.

- 1572 CE – 10,000 Protestants are slaughtered in France as heretics by Catholics

- 1586 CE – The entire female population of two villages in Germany are executed by the Inquisition

- 1610 CE – The Basque witch hunt begins

- 1692 CE – The Salem witch trials begin
- 1797 CE – A treaty written by George Washington's administration and ratified by the United States Senate states "The government of the United States is not, in any sense, founded on the Christian religion."

Religion has, since the foundation of Judaism, been a major cause for wars. This continues today when President Bush uses religion to justify his war in Iraq and proposed wars in Iran and elsewhere. It is important to realize that the United States has chosen as its enemies countries that are not Judeo-Christian in nature. This, however, does not mean that the other religions do not also use their holy books and scripture to pronounce war upon people that are not adherents to their ways as well. The Israeli occupation and domination of Palestine is certainly a clear example of using ancient scripture to get what you want. Citing god's promise that the "holy land" belongs to Israel, the Israeli's utilize many unlawful means to control the Palestinian people—including torture, imprisonment without representation, starvation, and economic strangulation.

At the same time, many Muslim leaders use Mohammed as an excuse to propose the elimination of the Jewish state and all other "non-believers."

We have already examined much of the Old Testament record of the Hebrew slaughter of the Canaanites as well as the Christian perversion of their religion and so we should briefly examine the Muslim thoughts towards non-Muslims. The Koran, in the Chapter of the Heifer reads: "Kill them wherever ye find them, and drive them out from whence they drive you out; for sedition is worse than slaughter; but fight them not by the Sacred Mosque until they fight you there; then kill them, for such is the recompense of those that misbelieve." [316]

We have witnessed the horrors of the Taliban in Afghanistan that forbade girls and women from being educated, punished men if their beards were not long enough, destroyed art and books and music and treasures of other times—all in the name of Allah. Likewise, we have witnessed conservative Christians who have sought to ban books, burn music and musical recording viewed as "Satanic," insisted on home schooling so that their children did not have to mix with the "other," attempted to stop certain subjects from being taught in public schools, have insisted that works of art depicting the nude form be either removed or covered up, and have caused the deaths of minorities and homosexuals because they are viewed as damned anyway.

There is, however, some hope. On October 11, 2007 130 Muslim scholars from around the world wrote a letter to Pope Benedict and other Christian leaders that the faiths must come together in peace and understanding.

The letter read, "If Muslims and Christians are not at peace, the world cannot be at peace. With the terrible weaponry of the modern world; with Muslims and Christians intertwined everywhere as never

---

[316] Palmer, E. H. trans. *The Koran*. London: Watkins Publishing 2007, 36.

before, no side can unilaterally win a conflict between more than half the world's inhabitants. Our common future is at stake. The very survival of the world is perhaps at stake." [317]

While the Pope received the letter, he did not care to comment on it at the time and it appeared that the Jews were not part of the mailing list.

---

[317] Graff, Peter. "Unprecedented Muslim call for peace with Christians". Reuters Limited, October 11, 2007.

Chapter Eight
Ethnic Cleansing and
God-Sponsored Slaughter

As we have seen, organized religion lends itself to the basest form of humanity. Whole populations are displaced, dominated and slaughtered in the name of god. In reality, it is not a religious reason but an excuse to take the property and the wealth, no matter how meager that wealth may be, and identity away from a particular group of people. While much of this book has focused on ancient cultures and events through the Middle Ages, we are daily faced with the same barbarity today for the same reasons. Today however it is not the Hebrews versus the Canaanites, it is the Hebrews versus the Muslims versus the Christians versus the Muslims.

The following is a summary of some of the more recent instances of religious "ethnic cleansing" since World War I. Of course, we do not ignore the Nazi's slaughtered millions of Jews, Pagans, Gypsies and others in World War II nor the ongoing incidents of genocide in Africa; however, these events are not entirely based on religion.

Turkey: (Muslims vs. Christians)

- 1914 – Muslim Turks disarmed the entire Armenian population, explaining that the Armenians were sympathetic to Christian Russia.

- April 24, 1915 – 300 Armenian educators, political leaders, writers, and clergy are arrested in Constantinople, tortured and then hanged or shot.

The caption on this photo reads "Hanged Armenian doctors…"

- Turkish soldiers and police as well as armed vigilantes conduct mass arrests of Christian Armenians. The men are tied together and then shot or bayoneted.

- Armenian women, children and the elderly are taken on death marches toward the Syrian desert.

- The abandoned homes and businesses belonging to the Armenians are taken over by Muslim Turks. Many of the Armenian children not killed are taken in by Turk families and forced to renounce their Christianity and convert to Islam. They are then given Turkish names.

- An estimated 1.5 million Armenians are killed in this religious "ethnic cleansing."

Yugoslavia: (Christians vs. Muslims)

- 1992 – The Christian Bosnian Serb Army formed, dislocating Muslim Croats, putting Muslims in detention camps, destroying Muslim villages.

- April 1992 – US and Europe recognizes the State of Bosnia, a Muslim nation. Serbs attack the Bosnian capital, Sarajevo, snipers kill over 3500 children alone. Mass shootings, deportations and roundup of Muslims undertaken. Concentration camps set up for men and boys. 8,000 men and boys between 12 and 60 years of age are selected and shot in Srebrenica, a UN "Safe Haven." Muslims are not allowed to work.

- August 1995 – US led NATO forces bomb Serbian positions, Muslim-Croat troops begin to retake part of the country.

- Over 200,000 Muslim civilians are killed, 20,000 missing and 2,000,000 become refugees.

A Muslim child lies shot by a Christian sniper as UN troops arrive to help.

Palestine: (Jews vs. Muslims)

- The State of Israel was created by United Nations mandate in 1948 after years of British rule. The people of Israel believe "the ancient, even biblical, association of the Jewish people with the Land of Israel was accepted in the Judeo-Christian tradition as a historical axiom" [318] and thus they have always been entitled to it.

- Israel believes that the area that is now identified as Israel had no identity prior to their arrival, that the land

---

[318] Gold, Dore and Jeffrey S. Helmreich. An Answer to the New Anti-Zionists: The Rights of the Jewish People to a Sovereign State in their Historic Homeland" in Jerusalem Viewpoints, No. 507   21 Heshvan 5764 / 16 November 2003 http://www.jcpa.org/jl/vp507.htm October 13, 2007.

was inhabited by a wide variety of non-heterogeneous people without a common heritage.

- Israel affirms that Israel during the Biblical period was in fact, Canaan. God "gives" this land to the Hebrews as an "inheritance" and God even defines the boundaries of the property (see Numbers 34:3).

- Palestine states that while Israel desires peace with its Palestinian residents, it is at a cost: "The only thing Israel has asked for, and continues to ask for in order to end the state of war with the Palestinians and its Arab neighbors, is that all recognize its right to be a racist state that discriminates by law against Palestinians and other Arabs and grants differential legal rights and privileges to its own Jewish citizens and to all other Jews anywhere." [319] Palestinian people believe that the land has been home of victims of "ethnic cleansing" for much longer than Israel has existed as a nation.

---

[319]Massad, Joseph. "Israel's Right to Be Racist."
http://www.palestineremembered.com/Articles/General/Story2289.html

Palestinians being forced from their home by Israeli troops in 1948.

- April 9, 1948 – Menachem Begin sends troops to the Palestinian village of Deir Yassin where 94 men, women and children are killed in an effort to "cleanse" the town. Twenty-four survivors are taken to Jerusalem "as trophies" and later taken back to Deir Yassin and shot. Today Jewish settlers occupy the village.

- May 25, 1948 – The village of al-Salihiyya totally destroyed.

- July 11, 1948 – 426 men, women and children are killed at al-Lydd. 176 of these are killed in the city's main mosque.

- October 29, 1948 – Over 100 men, women and children are killed at al-Dawayima and buried in the village well by Israeli soldiers. Only one village house remained standing after the operation was completed.

- October 29, 1948 – Israeli soldier shoot 70 blindfolded men and rape two women and a 14 year old girl. Most buildings destroyed and those that remain are occupied by Israeli settlers.

- June 7, 1967 – Three Palestinian villages totally destroyed by Israeli troops, being bulldozed and dynamited.

- Since the 1967 Arab-Israeli war, Israel has continued to destroy Palestinian villages, building Jewish towns over them. In addition, severe economic hardships are imposed on the Palestinians who are denied health care, employment, water and other necessities on a daily basis.

Israel's domination of Canaan continues today as it did when they first began their slaughter 4,000 years ago.

Genocide is, unfortunately, the result of our patriarchal religious tradition that has its roots in 4000 years of Biblical history. This common history among the Jews, Christians and Muslims creates an attitude that each is "Gods chosen" people and that they are permitted, even encouraged by God to do these terrible acts.

Afterword

It is not my intent to deny the existence of god or to tell those who believe in god in whatever manner they wish that they are wrong. I wish only to show that the god most of the world worships today is directly linked to that created when the Kurgan incursion swept out of the Russian steppes and overran the known world from Central Asia to the Indus Valley to Old Europe and the Mediterranean.

The god of today is invoked as he was in ancient times—to validate ethnic cleansing, to substantiate claims to vast areas of land and resources, to repudiate other religions and to foster "patriotic" wars. In short, to make the world over in the image of a world spiraling out of control with blood lust rather than peace as the goal. This is an image those original nomadic warriors envisioned, created for themselves and gave to us as their heritage.

It is unfortunate that three potentially great religions, all based in the same theology, have created such hatred and suffering in the world. Much suffering is imposed as well by individual groups such as certain evangelical churches and their congregations who often demonstrate against homosexuals and by extremist groups such as the Aryan Brotherhood, Nazi's and Ku Klux Klan who terrorize with the belief that they are doing what God requires of them.

The United States government, which, to the horror of its founding fathers, has become a theocracy, also acts out in the name of religion, refusing to sign laws that offer equal protection to homosexuals, warring against Muslim states and exploiting the environment to the point of certain extinction for certain creatures and habitats. Education and health care have become of little concern when they interfere with profits and "Christian ideals" and helping minority communities recover from disaster is an afterthought. It also continues the conflicts between Israel, Palestinians and Arab nations because the government embraces the Jewish state as God's people and allows illegal acts to proceed by arming Israel and vetoing any United Nations resolution that may help the international situation.

Christianity and Judaism continue to dominate the world in ways that may ultimately bring about its destruction.

The "Christian" view of homosexuals.

About the Author

Gary R. Varner has written a number of books on folklore, mythology and early religions. He has contributed to a number of scholarly periodicals as well, including *Living Spring Journal* (UK) and *Magister Botanicus* (Germany). He is a member of the American Folklore Society and the Foundation for Mythological Studies and has been listed in a number of editions of *Who's Who in America* and *Who's Who in the World.*

Currently living in Northern California, the author invites interested readers to visit him on his website at www.authorsden.com/garyrvarner.

Selected Bibliography

Andrews, Tamra. *A Dictionary of Nature Myths: Legends of the Earth, Sea, and Sky.* Oxford: Oxford University Press 1998

Baring, Anne and Jules Cashford. *The Myth of the Goddess: Evolution of An Image.* London: Arkana/Penguin Books 1993

Beckwith, Martha. *Hawaiian Mythology.* Honolulu: University of Hawaii Press 1970 (A reprint of the 1940 edition published by Yale University Press)

Biedermann, Hans. *Dictionary of Symbolism: Cultural Icons & The Meanings Behind Them.* New York: Meridian Books 1994

Bierhorst, John. *The Mythology of Mexico and Central America.* New York: William Morrow and Company, Inc. 1990

Black, Jeremy and Anthony Green. *Gods, Demons and Symbols of Ancient Mesopotamia.* Austin: University of Texas Press 1992

Brewster, Harry. *The River Gods of Greece: Myths and Mountain Waters in the Hellenic World.* London: I.B. Tauris Publishers 1997

Bryant, Page. *Awakening Arthur!* London: The Aquarian Press 1991

Budge, Sir Wallis. *Egyptian Religion.* New York: Bell Publishing Company 1959

Burkert, Walter. *Ancient Mystery Cults.* Cambridge: Harvard University Press 1987

Carmichael, Joel. *The Birth of Christianity: Reality and Myth.* New York: Dorset Press 1989

Campbell, Joseph. *Creative Mythology: The Masks of God Volume IV.* London: Secker & Warburg 1968

Charbonneau-Lassay, Louis. *The Bestiary of Christ.* New York: Arkana/Penguin Books 1992

Cirlot, J.E.*A Dictionary of Symbols.* 2nd ed., New York: Barnes & Noble Books 1995

Cooper, D. Jason. *Mithras: Mysteries and Initiation Rediscovered.* York Beach: Samuel Weiser, Inc. 1996

Cooper, J.C. *An Illustrated Encyclopaedia of Traditional Symbols.* London: Thames & Hudson Ltd. 1978

Cotterell, Arthur. The Encyclopedia of Mythology: Classical, Celtic, Greek. London: Hermes House 2005

Cowan, James G. The Elements of the Aborigine Tradition. Shaftsbury: Element Books Limited 1992

D'Alviella, Count Goblet. *The Migration of Symbols.* New York: University Books 1956

Doresse, Jean. *The Secret Books of the Egyptian Gnostics.* New York: MJF Books 1986

Eisler, Riane. *The Chalice & The Blade: Our History, Our Future.* San Francisco: HarperSanFrancisco 1987

Eliade, Mircea. *Shamanism: Archaic Techniques of Ecstasy.* Princeton University Press 1964

Ellerbe, Hellen. *The Dark Side of Christian History.* Orlando: Morningstar and Lark 1995

Ely, Talfourd. *The Gods of Greece and Rome.* Mineola: Dover Publications Inc. 2003 (A reprint of the 1891 edition published by G.P. Putnam's Sons)

Fiske, John. *Myths and Myth-Makers: Old Tales and Superstitions Interpreted by Comparative Mythology.* Boston: Houghton, Mifflin and Company 1881

Gadon, Elinor W. *The Once and Future Goddess.* San Francisco: Harper & Row, Publishers 1989

Gimbutas, Marija. *The Language of the Goddess.* San Francisco: HarperSanFrancisco 1991

Gimbutas, Marija. *The Civilization of the Goddess: The World of Old Europe.* San Francisco: HarperSanFrancisco 1991

Graves, Kersey. *The World's Sixteen Crucified Saviors.* Kempton: Adventures Unlimited Press 2001. A reprint of the 1875 publication.

Gray, John. *Archaeology and the Old Testament World.* Edinburgh: Thomas Nelson and Sons LTD. 1962

Halley, Henry. *Halley's Bible Handbook.* Grand Rapids: Zondervan Publishing House 1965

Howells, William. *The Heathens: Primitive Man and His Religions.* Garden City: Anchor Books 1962

Hutton, Ronald. The Pagan Religions of the Ancient British Isles: Their Nature and Legacy. Oxford: Blackwell 1993

Inman, Thomas. *Ancient Pagan and Modern Christian Symbolism.* New York: Cosimo Classics 2005

James, E.O. *The Ancient Gods.* Edison: Castle Books 2004

Johnson, Buffie. *Lady of the Beasts.* Rochester: Inner Traditions International 1994

Kostof. Spiro. A History of Architecture: Settings and Ritual. Oxford: Oxford University Press 1985

Leeming, David Adams. *The World of Myth*. New York: Oxford University Press 1990

Leisegang, Hans. "The Mystery of the Serpent" in *Pagan and Christian Mysteries: Papers from the Eranos Yearbook*, edited by Joseph Campbell. New York: The Bollingen Foundation/Harper & Row Publishers 1955

Lewis, Brenda Ralph. *Ritual Sacrifice: Blood and Redemption*. Phoenix Mill: Sutton Publishing Limited 2006

Mackenzie, Donald A. *Crete & Pre-Hellenic Myths and Legends*. London: Senate 1995 (A reprint of the 1917 publication by the Gresham Publishing Company, London)

Mackenzie, Donald A. *Ancient Man in Britain*. London: Senate 1996. (A reprint of the 1922 edition published by Blackie & Son Limited, London)

Mallory, J.P. *In Search of the Indo-Europeans: Language, Archaeology and Myth*. New York: Thames and Hudson 1989

Markale, Jean. *The Great Goddess: Reverence of the Devine Feminine From the Paleolithic to the Present*. Rochester: Inner Traditions 1999

Maringer, Johannes. *The Gods of Prehistoric Man: History of Religion*. London: Phoenix Press 2002

Mercantante, Anthony S. *Good and Evil in Myth & Legend*. New York: Barnes & Noble Books 1996

Mbiti, John S. *African Religions and Philosophy*. New York: Anchor Books 1969

Mohen, Jean-Pierre. *Prehistoric Art: The Mythical Birth of Humanity*. Paris: Telleri 2002

Oakes, Lorna and Lucia Gahlin. *Ancient Egypt*. New York: Barnes & Noble Books 2006

O'Connell, Mark and Raje Airey. *The Complete Encyclopedia of Signs & Symbols*. London: Hermes House 2005

O'Grady, Joan. *The Prince of Darkness: The Devil in History, Religion and the Human Psyche*. New York: Barnes and Noble Books 1989

Palmer, E. H. trans. *The Koran*. London: Watkins Publishing 2007

Patai, Raphael. *The Hebrew Goddess*. New York: Avon Books 1978

Philpot, Mrs. J.H. *The Sacred Tree in Religion and Myth*. Mineola: Dover Publications, Inc. 2004 (A reprint of the 1897 edition published by Macmillan and Co. Ltd, London and New York)

Porteous, Alexander. *The Lore of the Forest: Myths and Legends*. London: Senate 1996

Romer, John. *Testament: The Bible and History*. Old Saybrook: Konecky & Konecky 1988

Ross, Anne. *Folklore of the Scottish Highlands*. Gloucestershire: Tempus Publishing LTD. 2000

Schwartz, Howard. *Lilith's Cave*. Oxford: Oxford University Press 1988

Skinner, Fred Gladstone. *Myths and Legends of the Ancient Near East*. New York: Barnes and Noble Books 1970

Spence. Lewis. *Ancient Egyptian Myths and Legends*. New York: Dover Publications, Inc. 1990

Stark, Rodney. *Discovering God: The Origins of the Great Religions and the Evolution of Belief*. New York: HarperCollins 2007

Stone, Merlin. *When God Was A Woman.* New York: Barnes & Noble Books 1993

Toorawa, Shawkat M. "Khidr: The History of a Ubiquitous Master" in *Sufi Selected Article,* Issue Number 30, Published by Khaniqahi Mimatullahi Publications 2000

Tresidder, Jack. *Symbols and their Meanings.* New York: Barnes & Noble 2006

Unterman, Alan. *Dictionary of Jewish Lore & Legend.* New York: Thames and Hudson 1991

Walker, Barbara G. *The Women's Encyclopedia of Myths and Secrets.* Edison: Castle Books 1996

Walter, Philippe. *Christianity: The origins of a Pagan Religion.* Rochester: Inner Traditions 2006

Waugh, Alexander. *God.* New York: St. Martin's Press 2002

Wilkinson, Richard H. *The Complete Gods and Goddesses of Ancient Egypt.* London: Thames and Hudson 2003

Wolkstein, Diane and Samuel Noah Kramer. *Inanna: Queen of Heaven and Earth.* New York: Harper & Row, Publishers 1983

Zimmer, Heinrich. *Myths and Symbols in Indian Art and Civilization.* Princeton: Princeton University Press-Bollinger Series VI, 1946

Index

GODS OF MAN

GODS OF MAN

GODS OF MAN

GODS OF MAN